Gentle Symmetry: An Adult Coloring Book

Joshua Guess

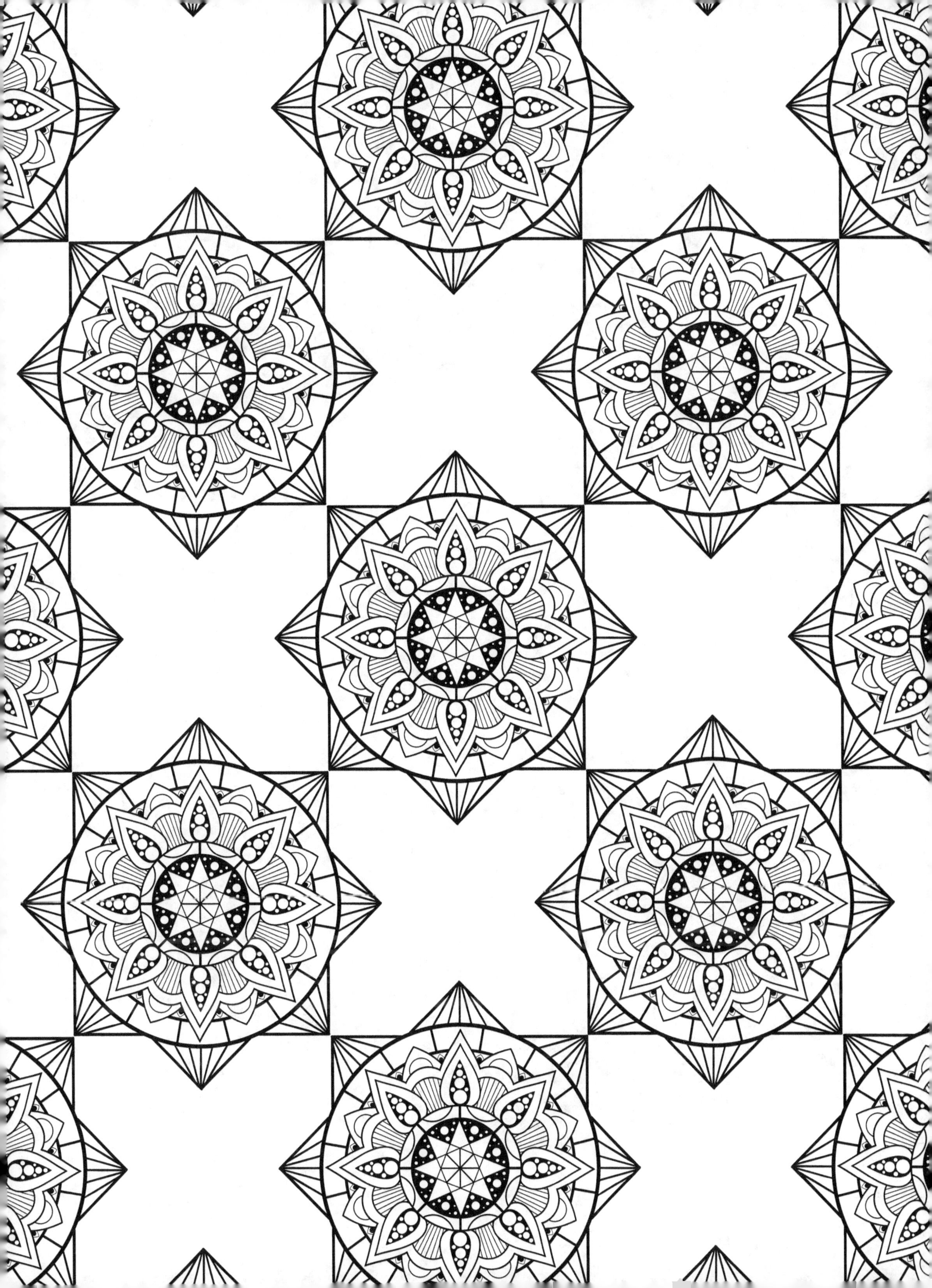

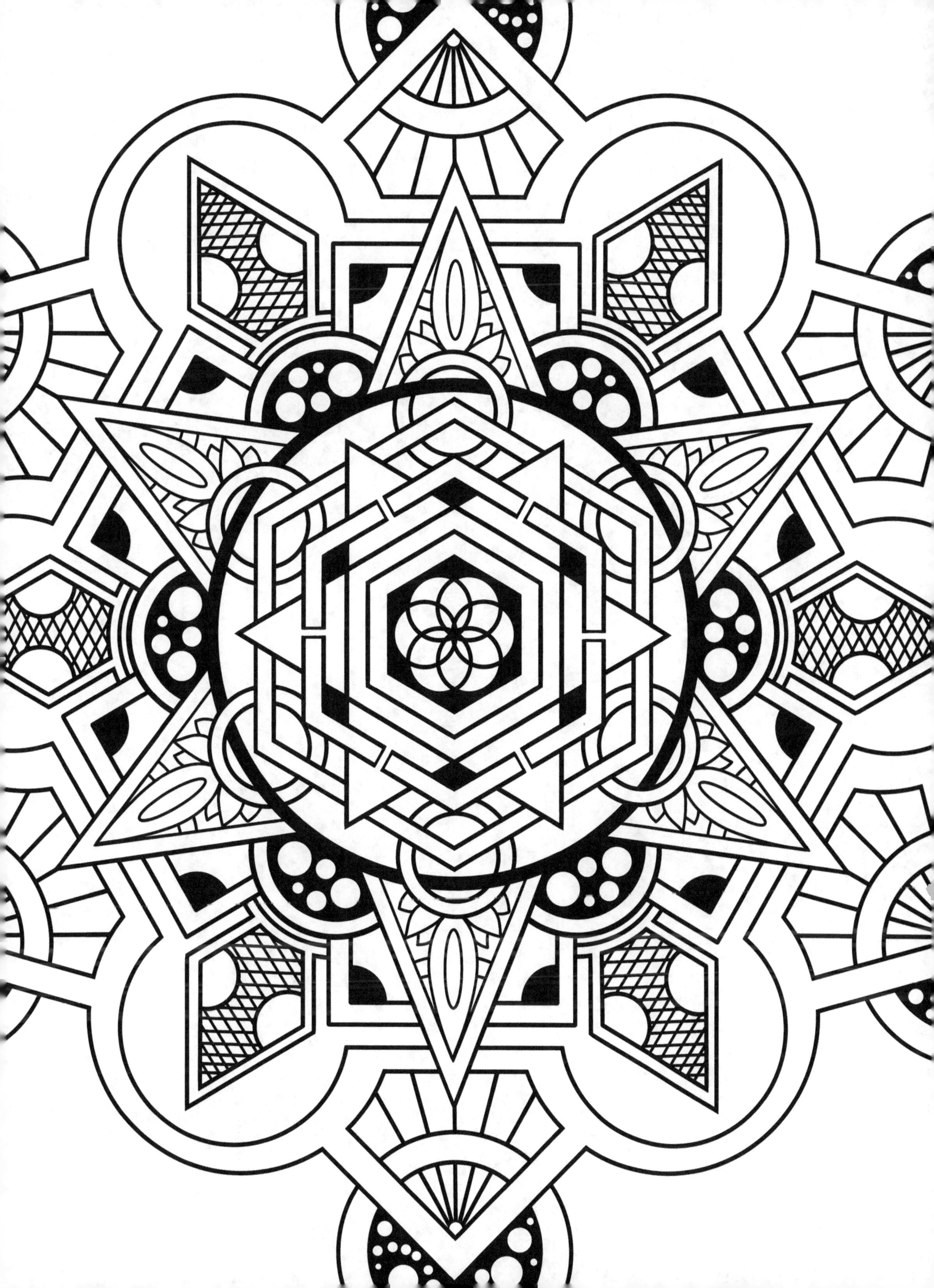

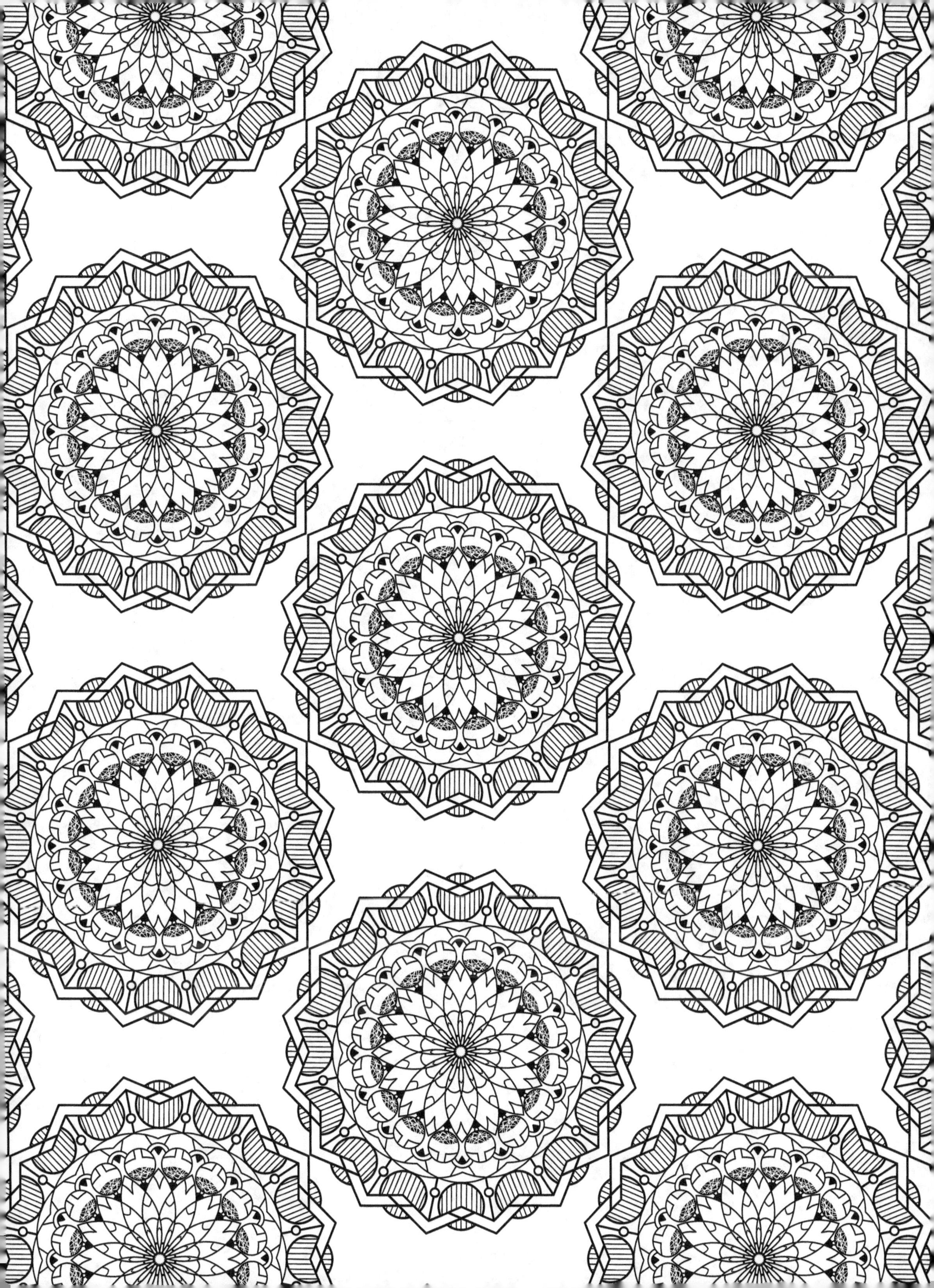

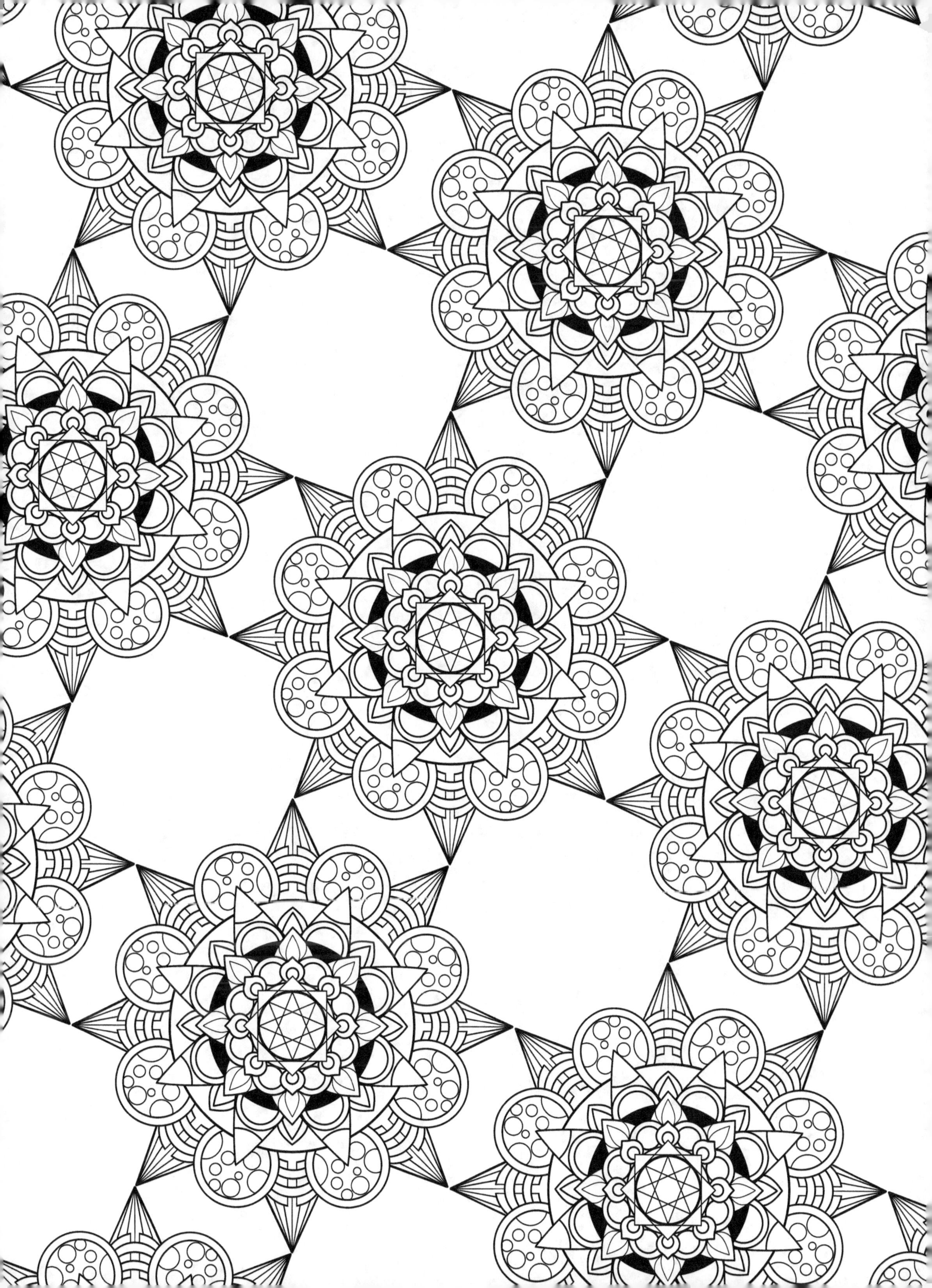

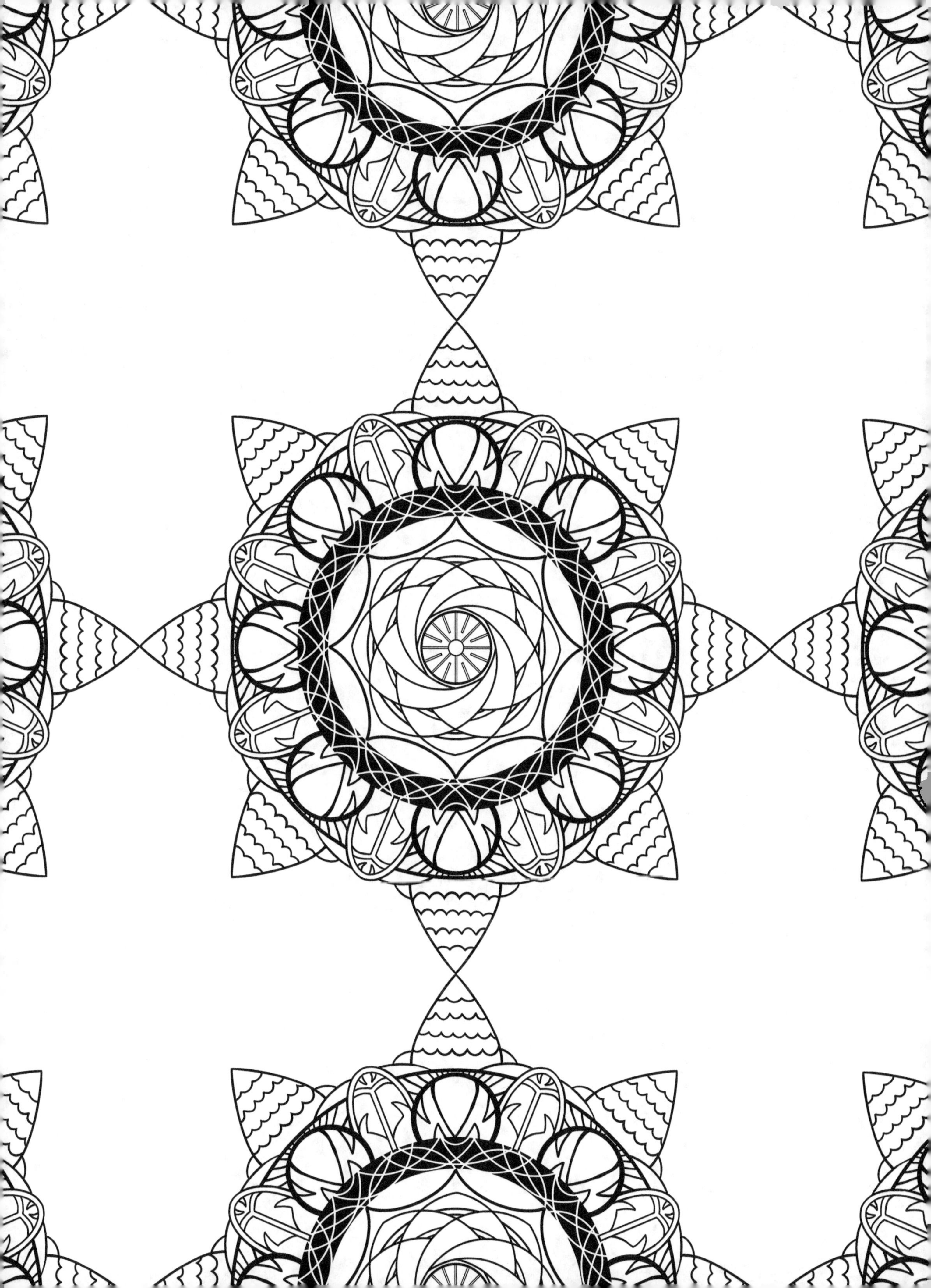

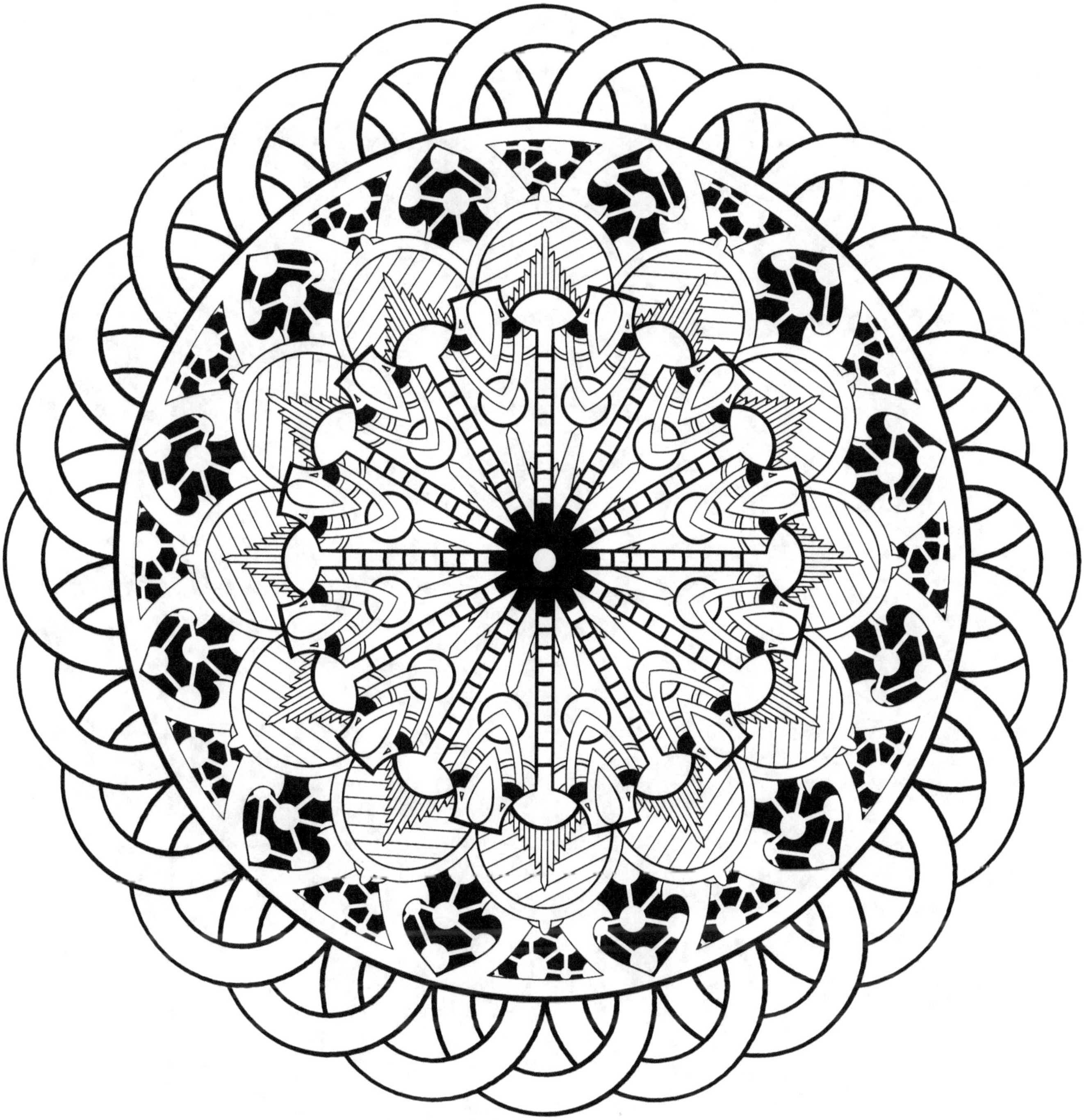

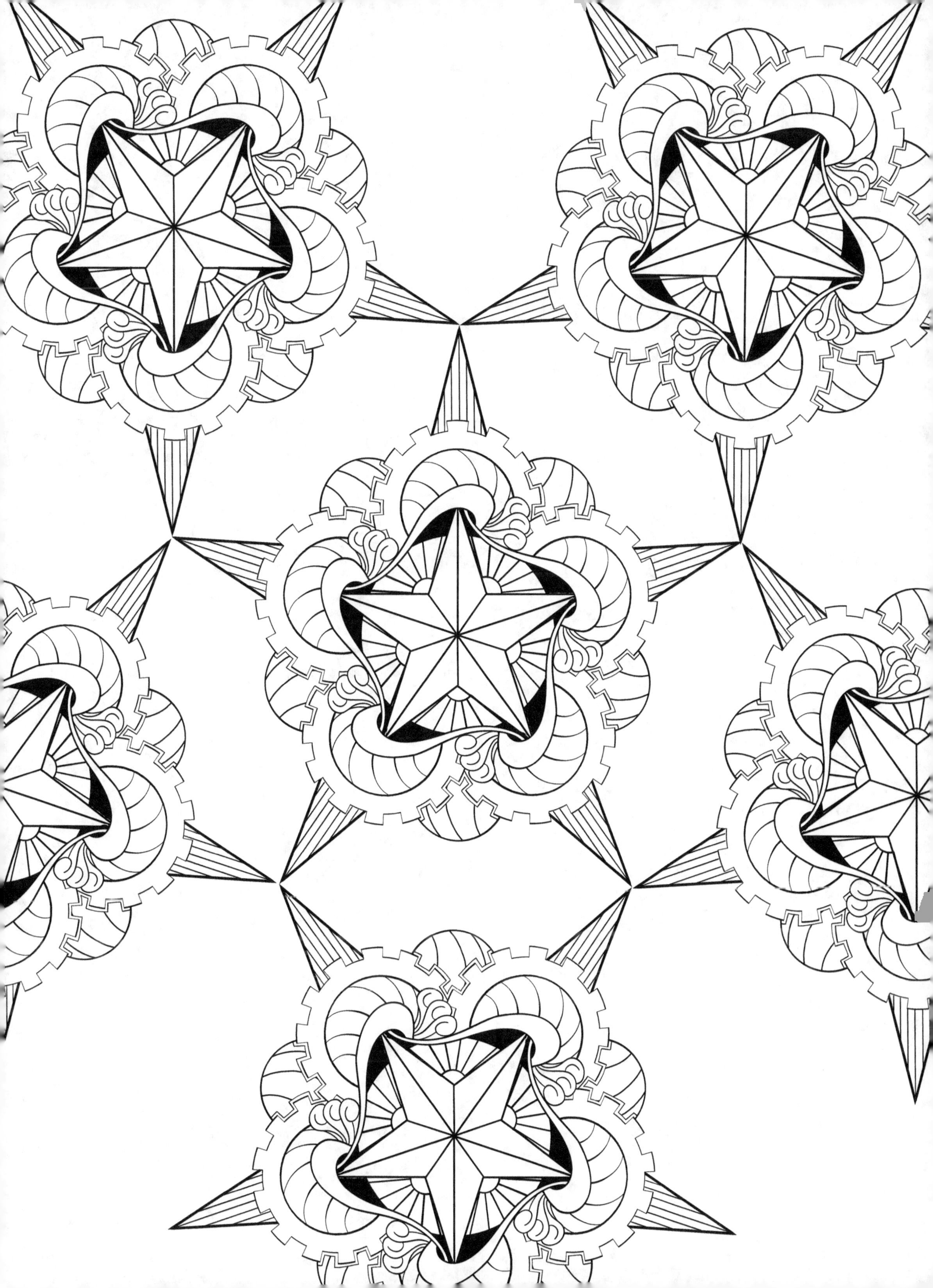

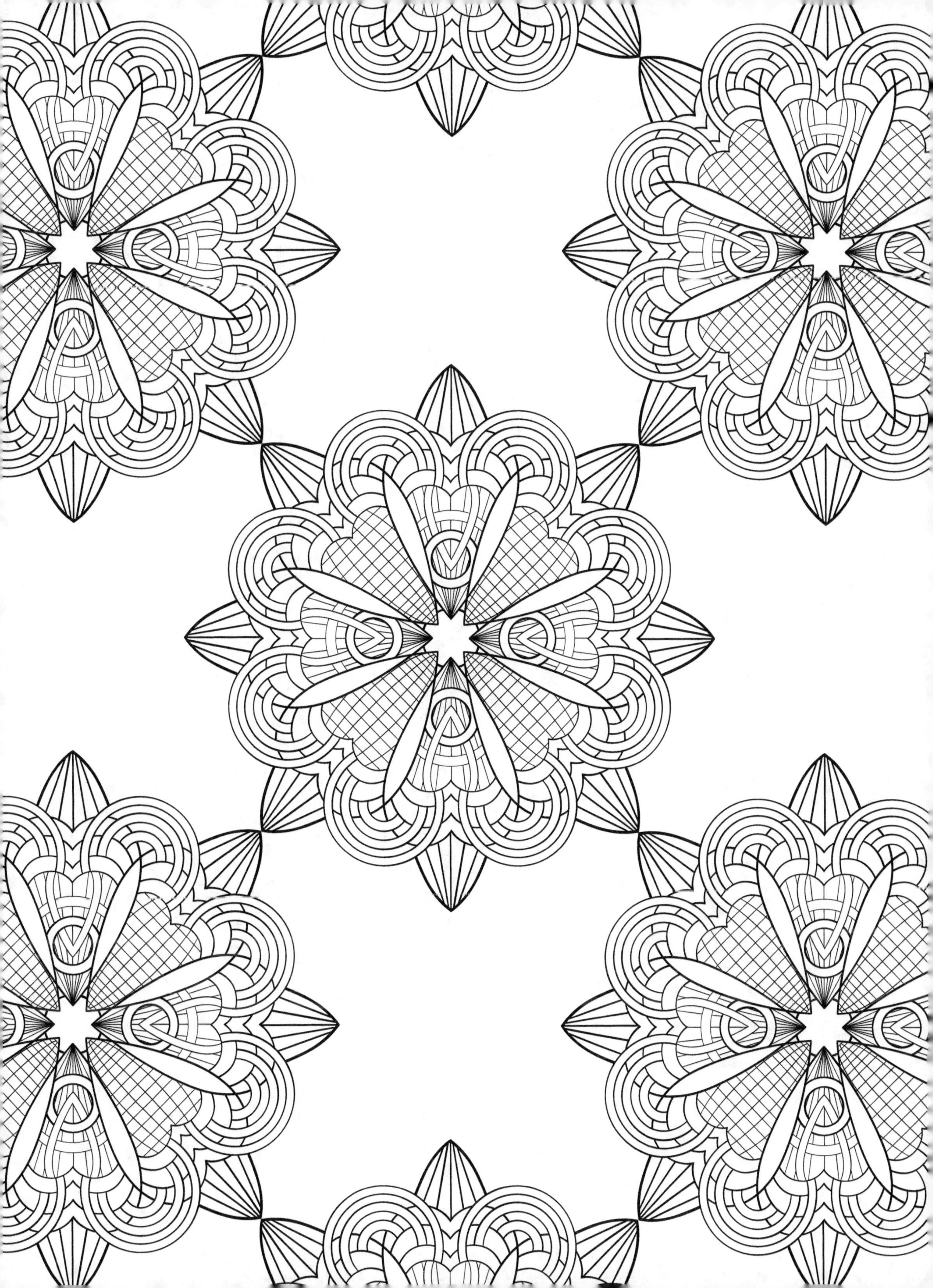

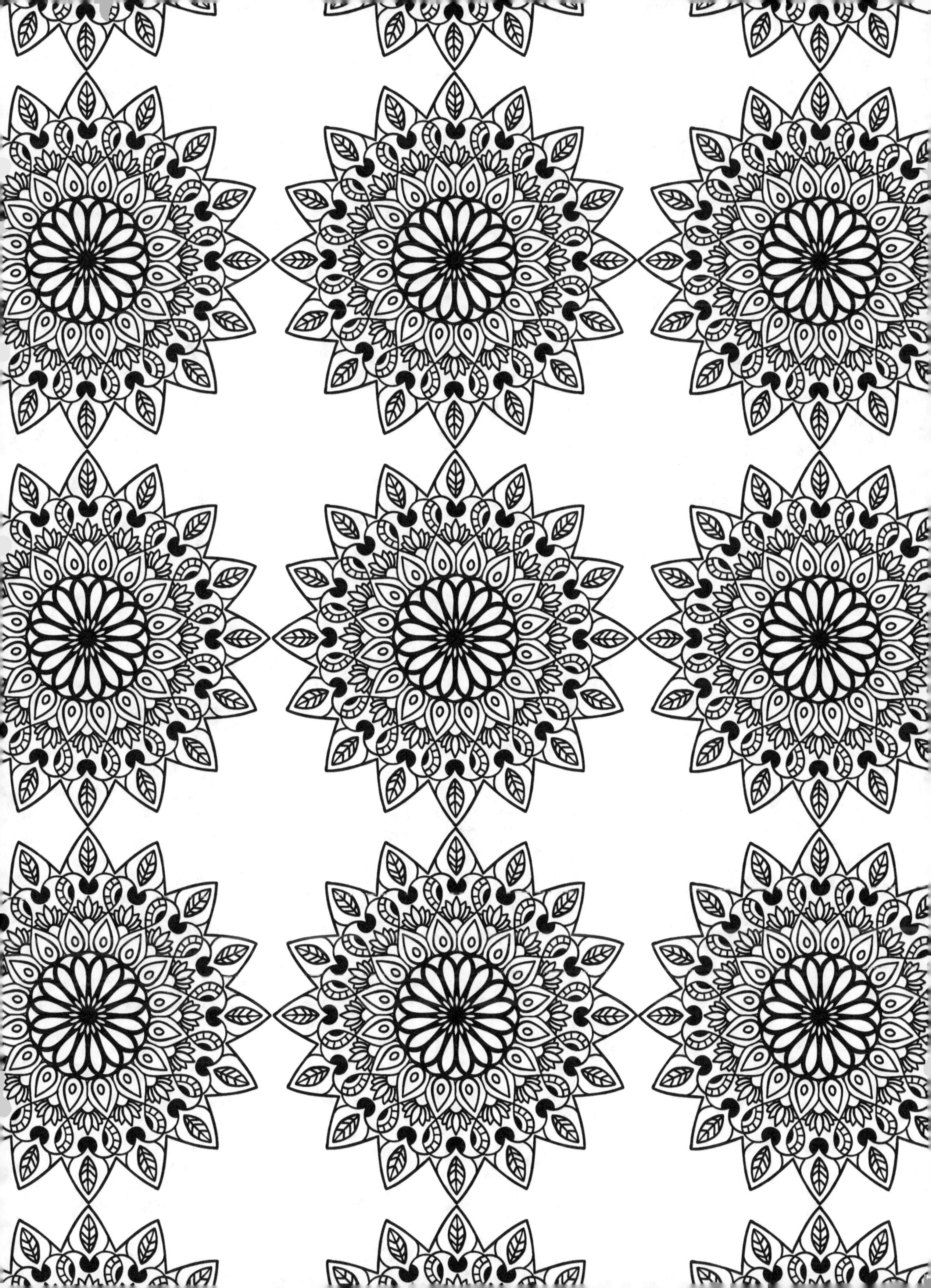

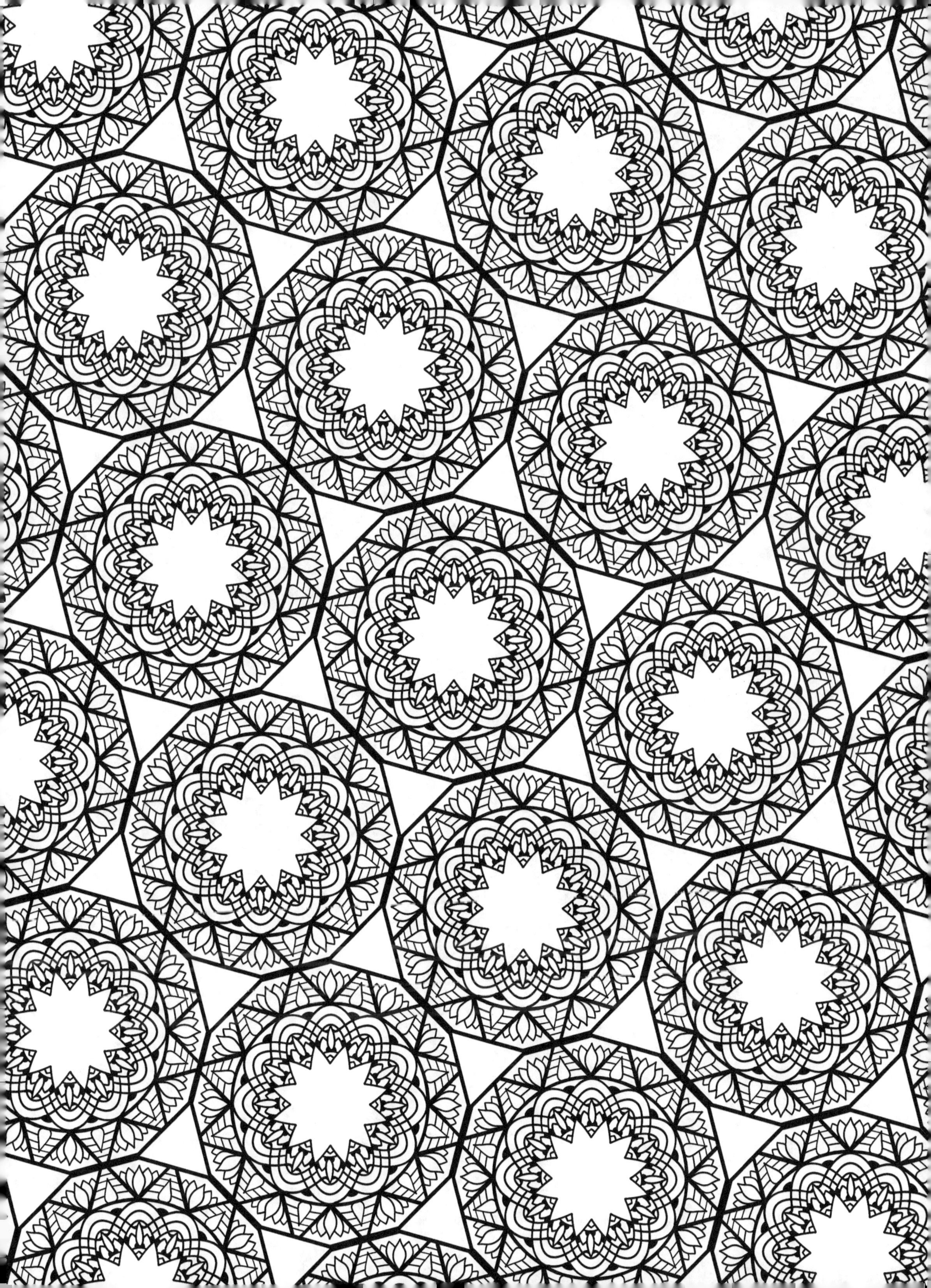

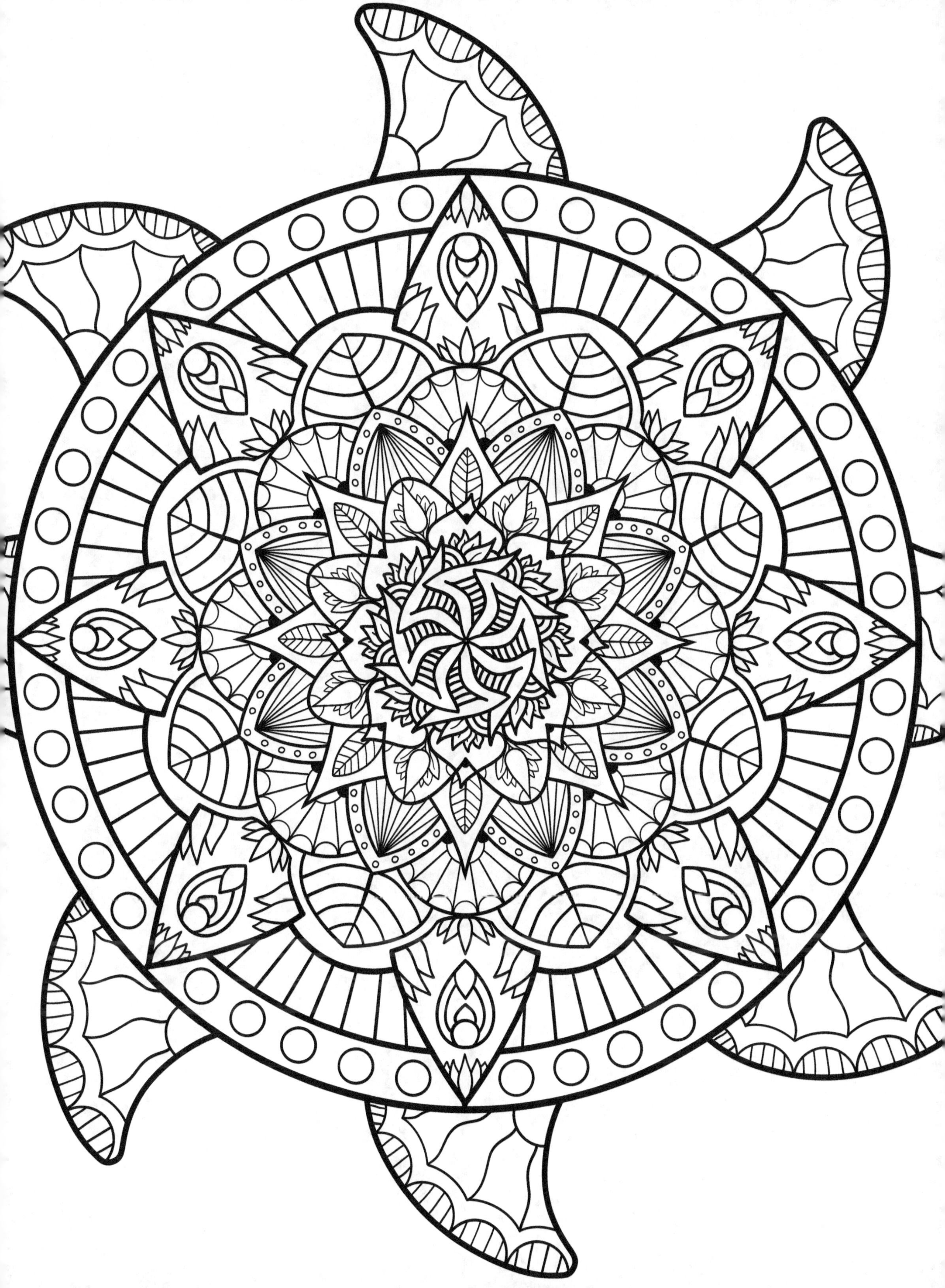

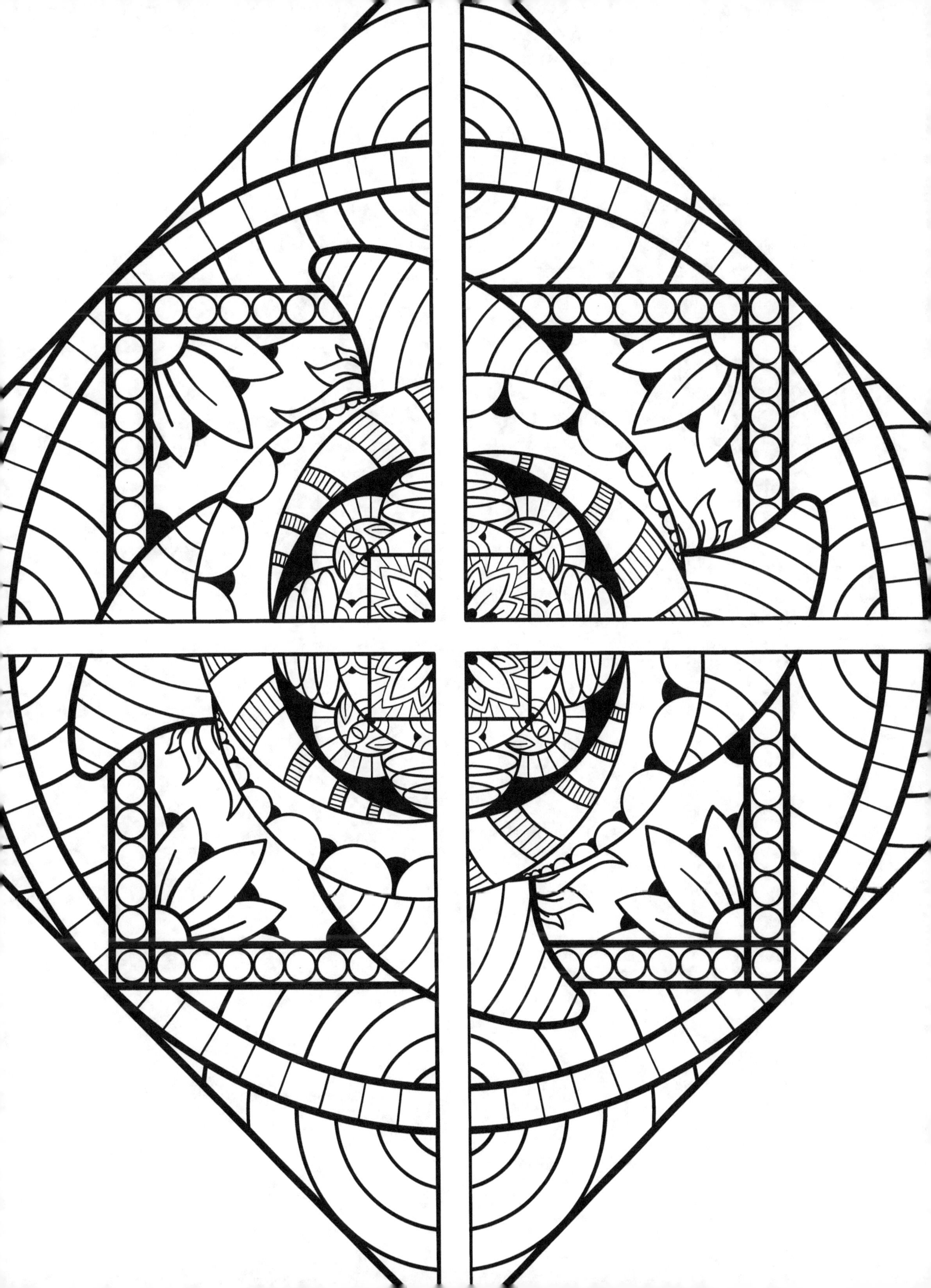

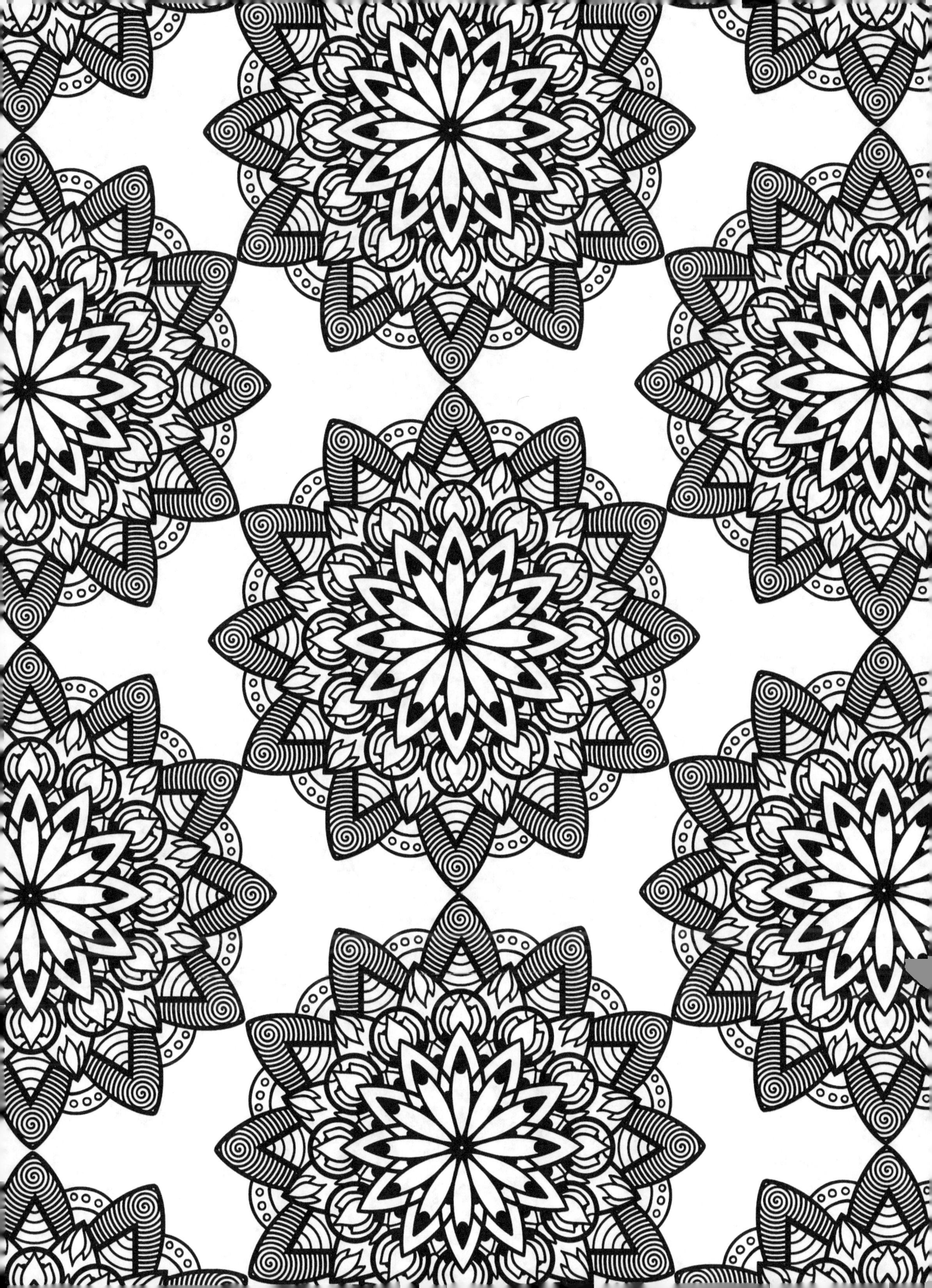

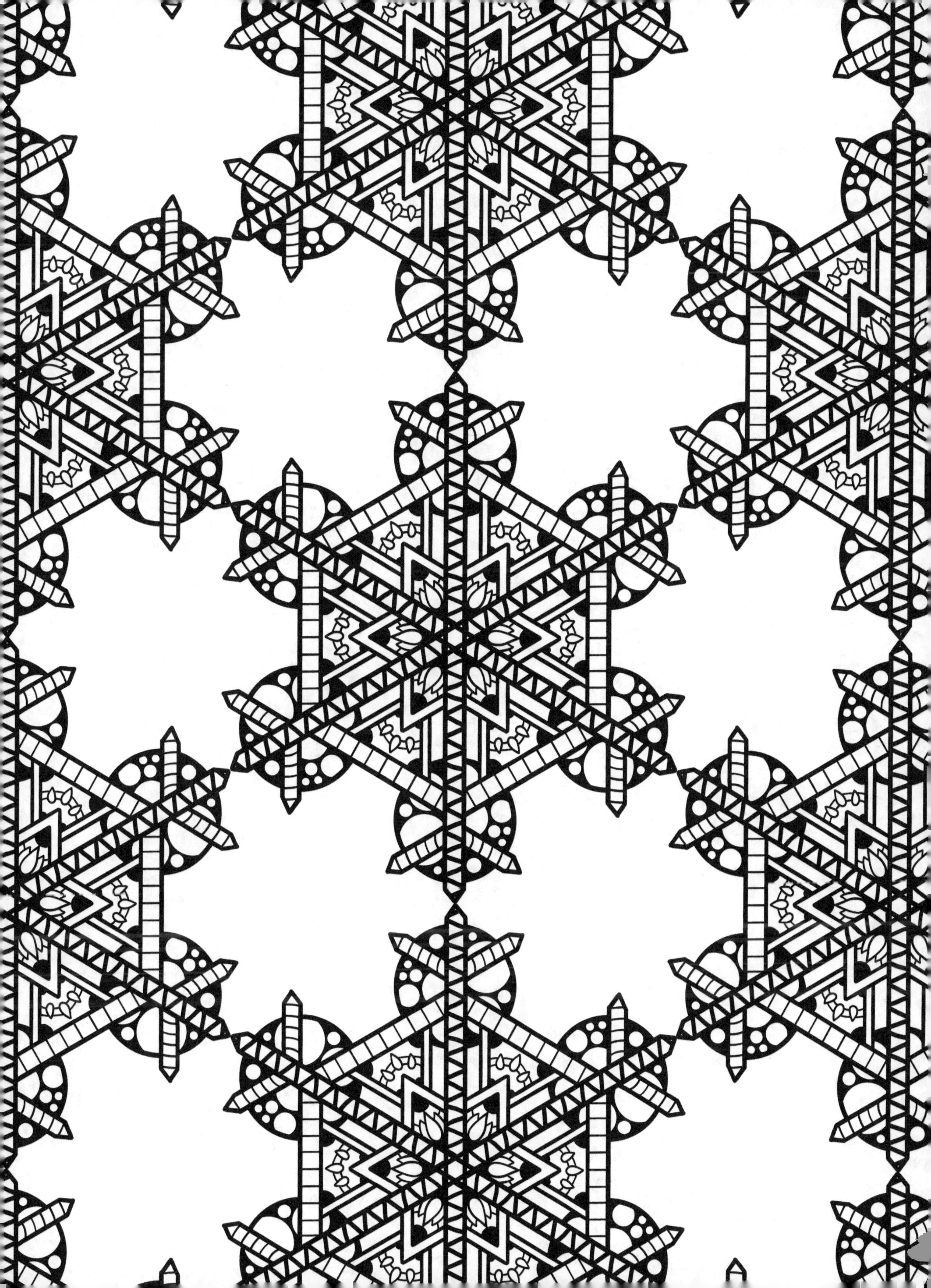

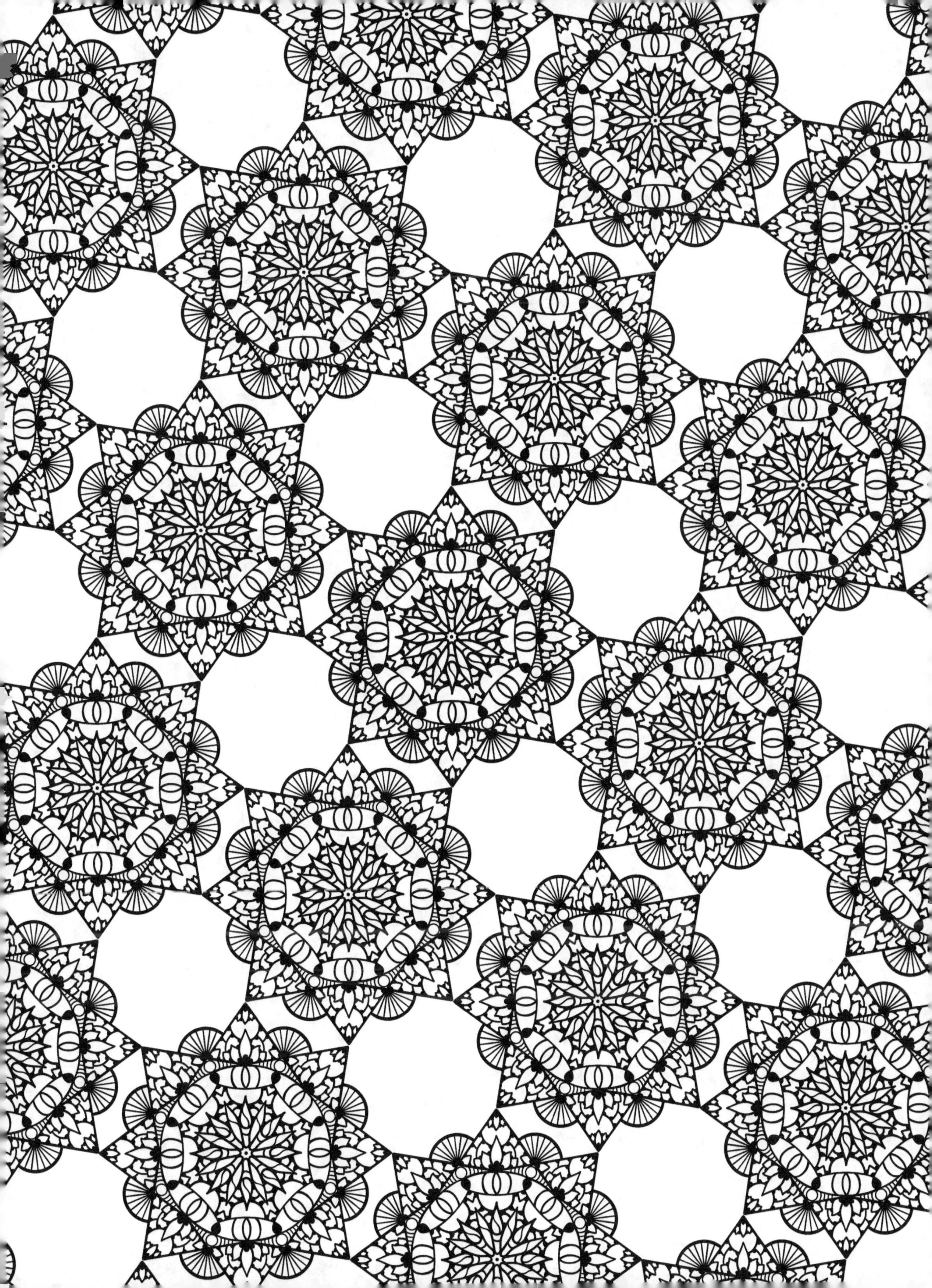

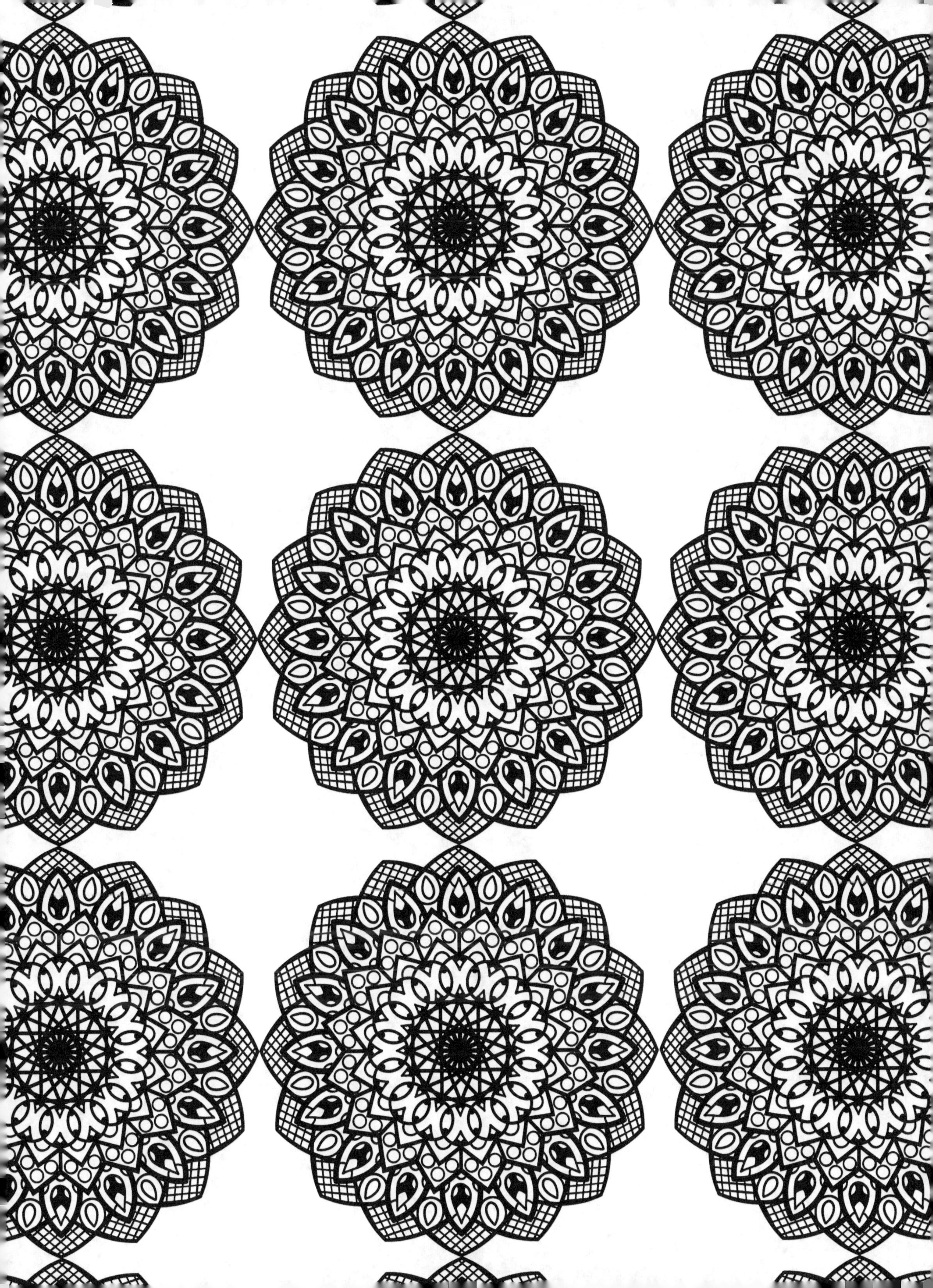

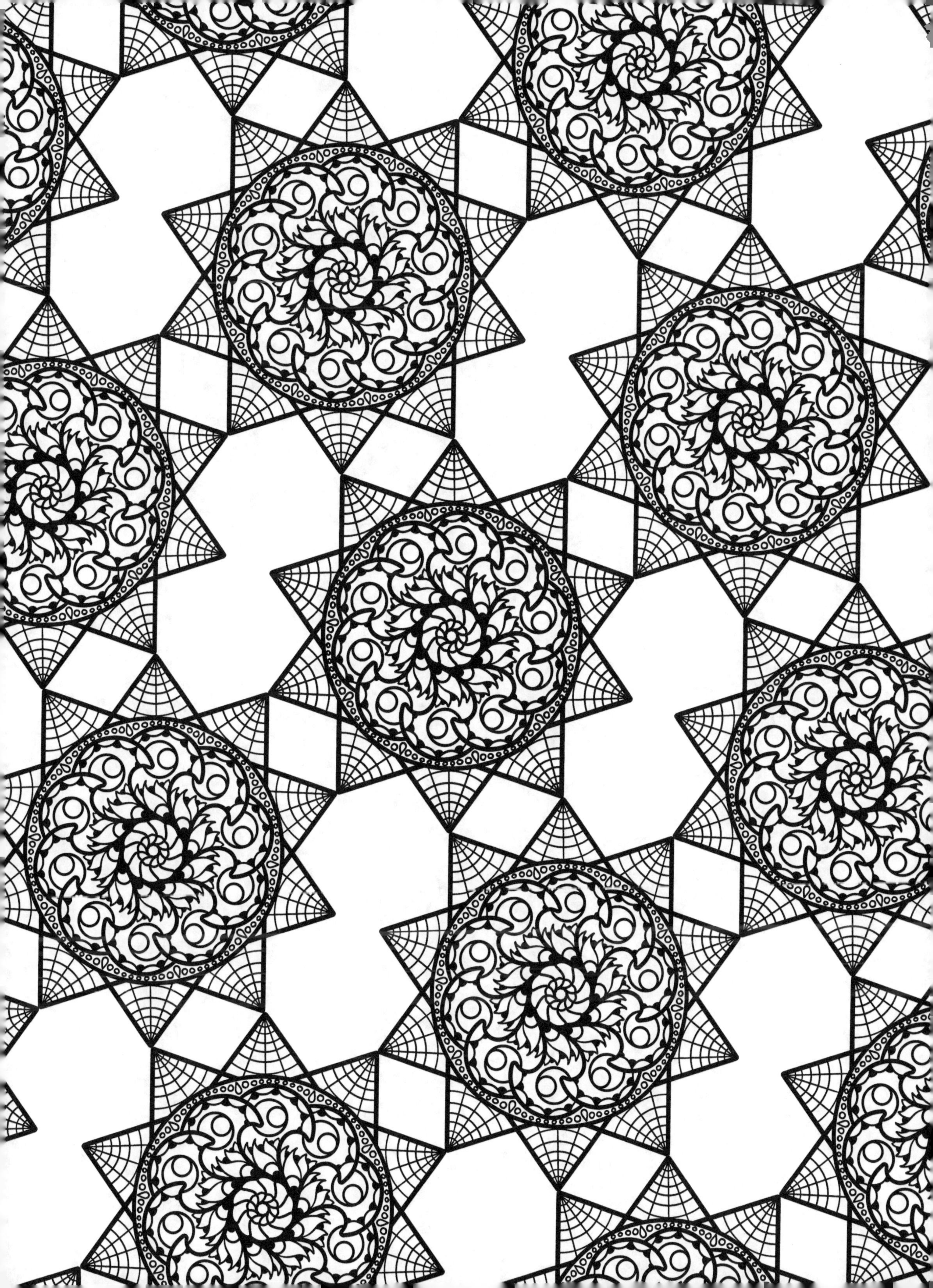

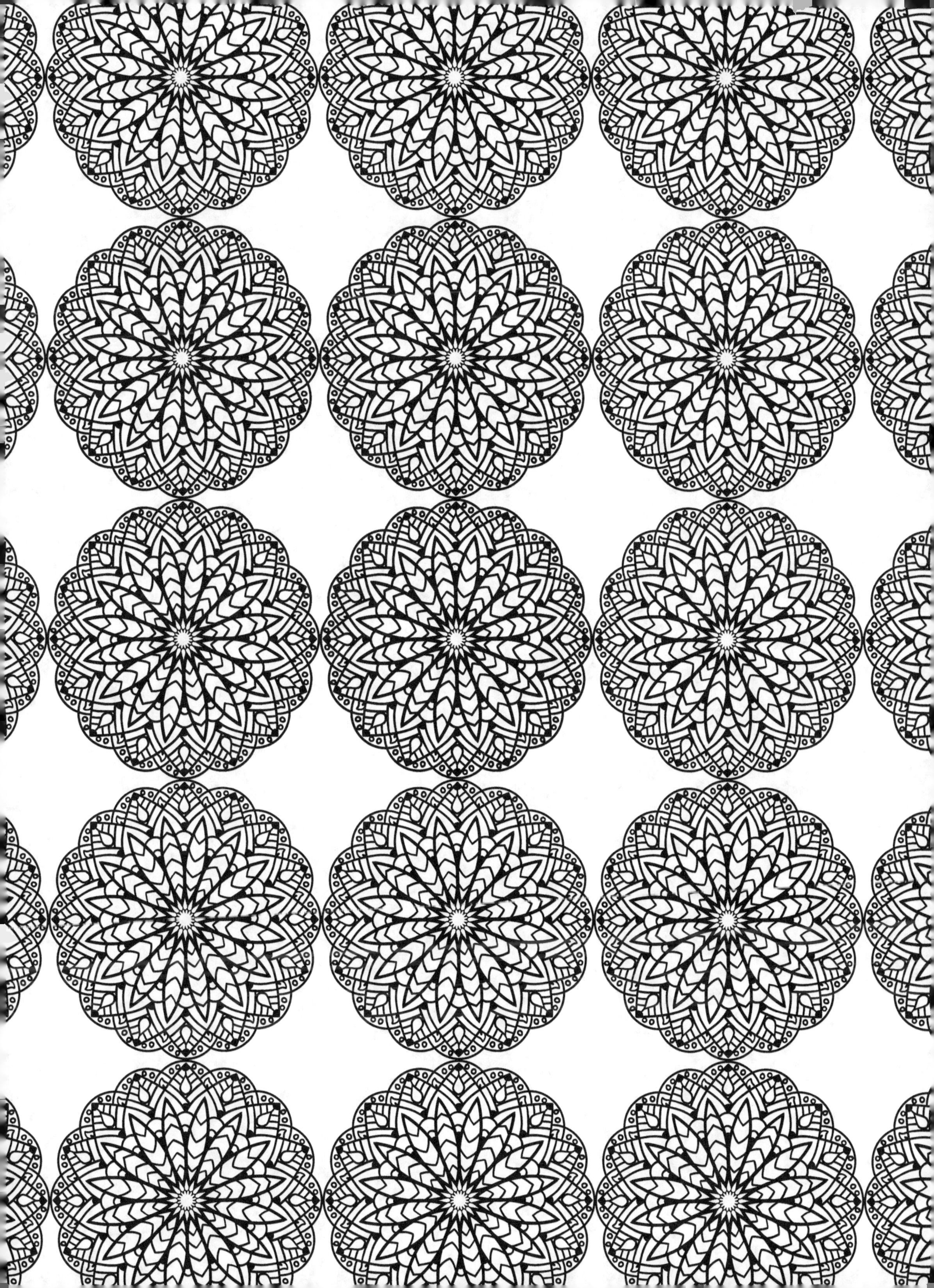

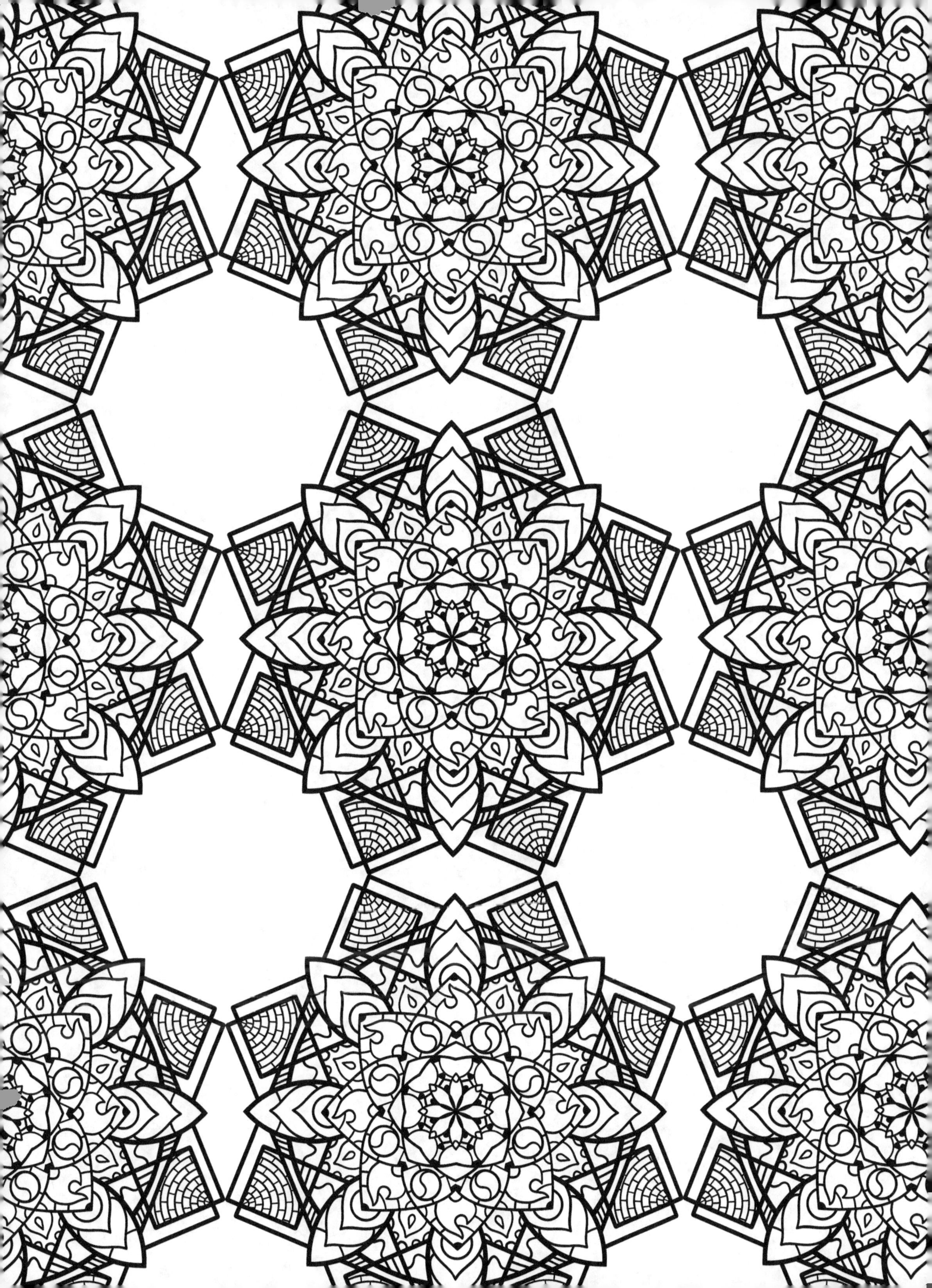

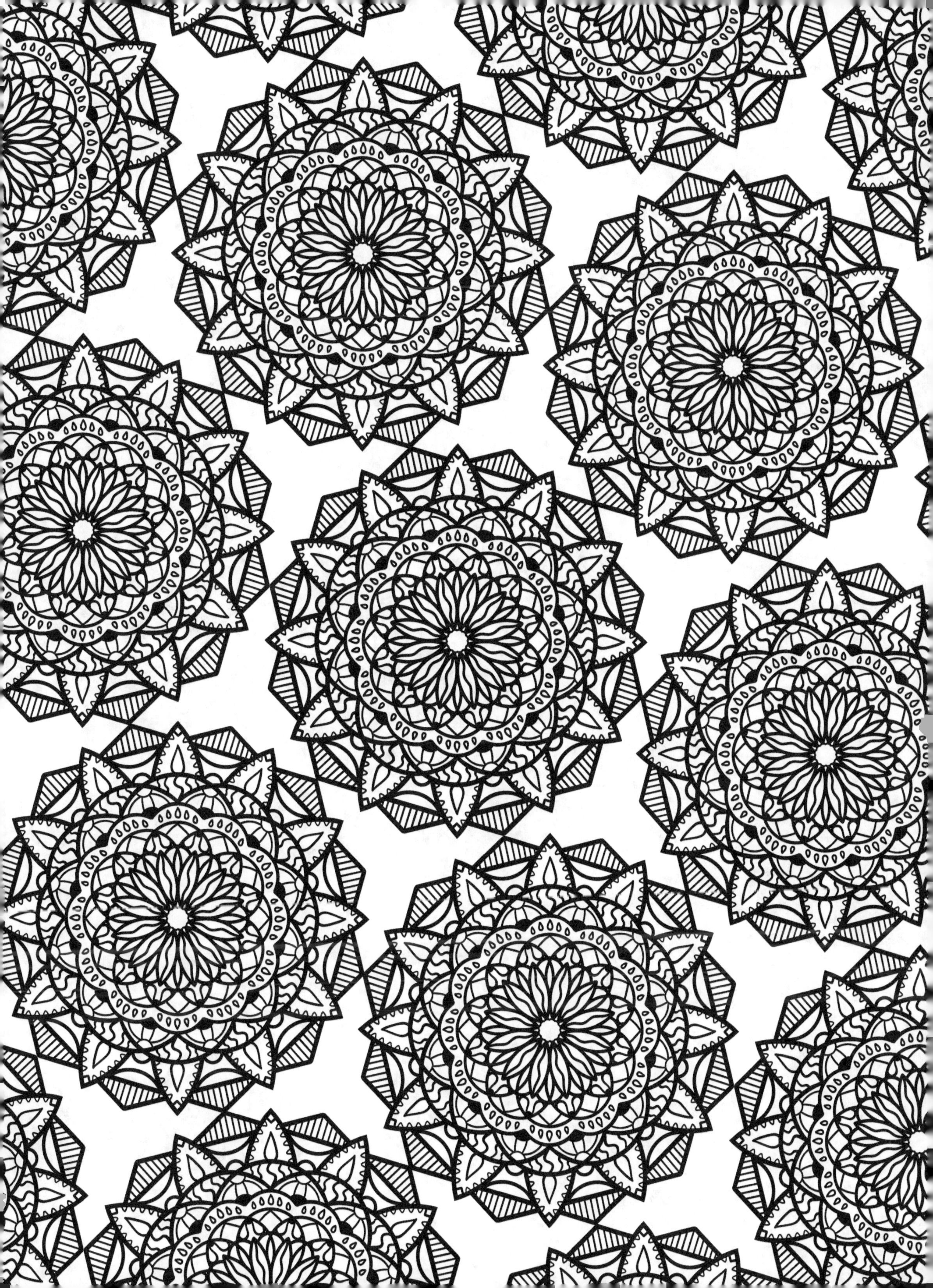

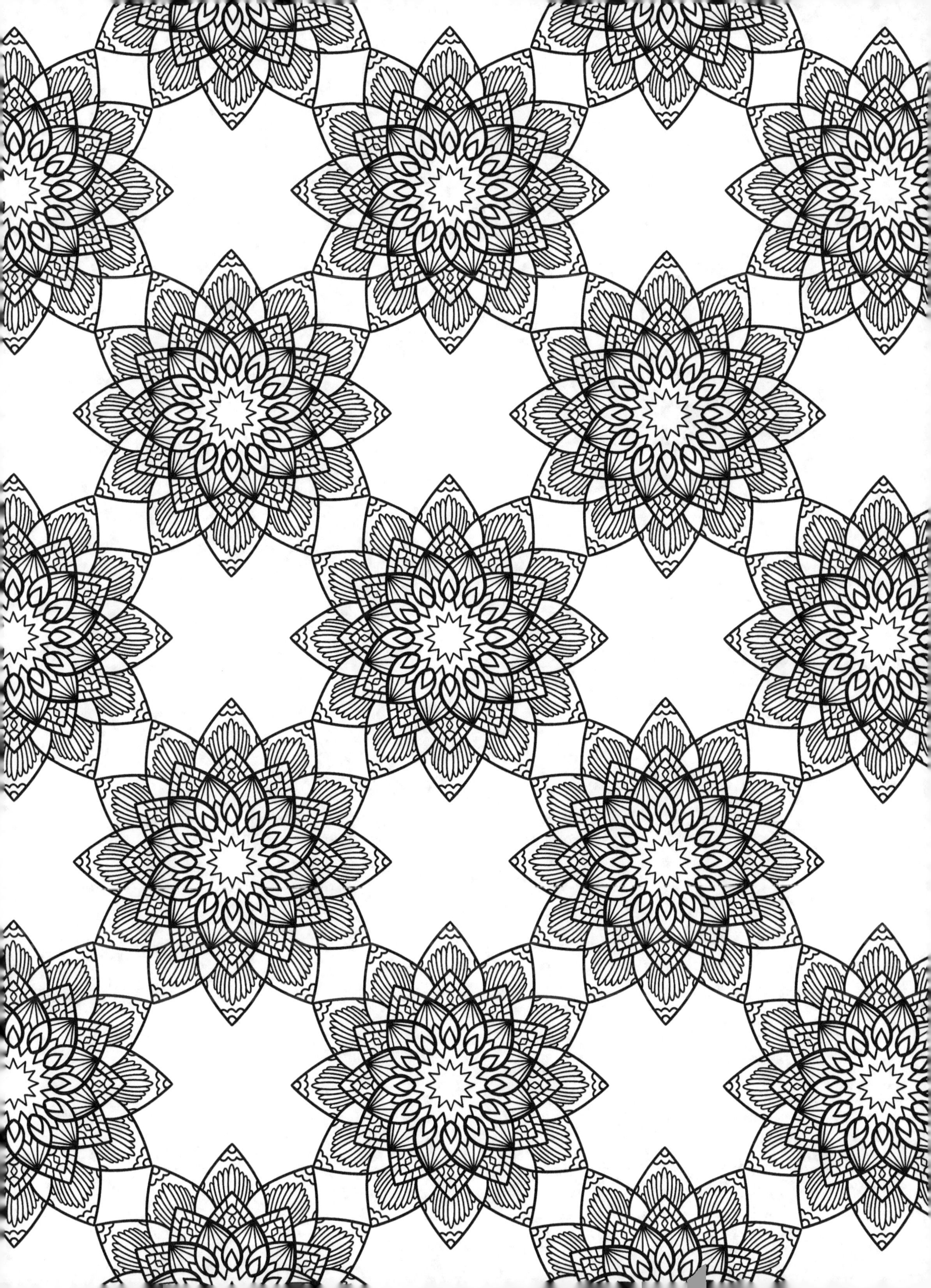

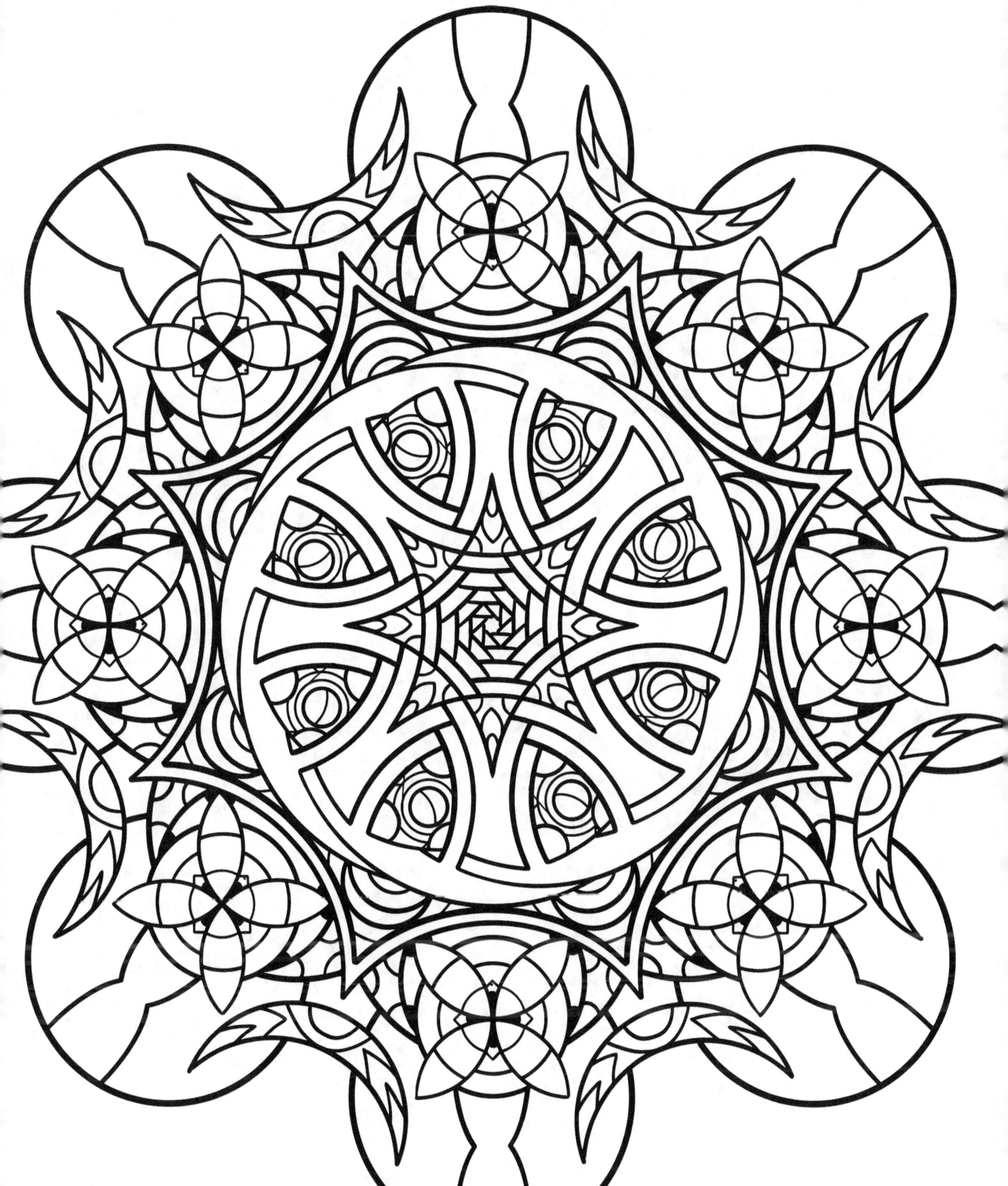

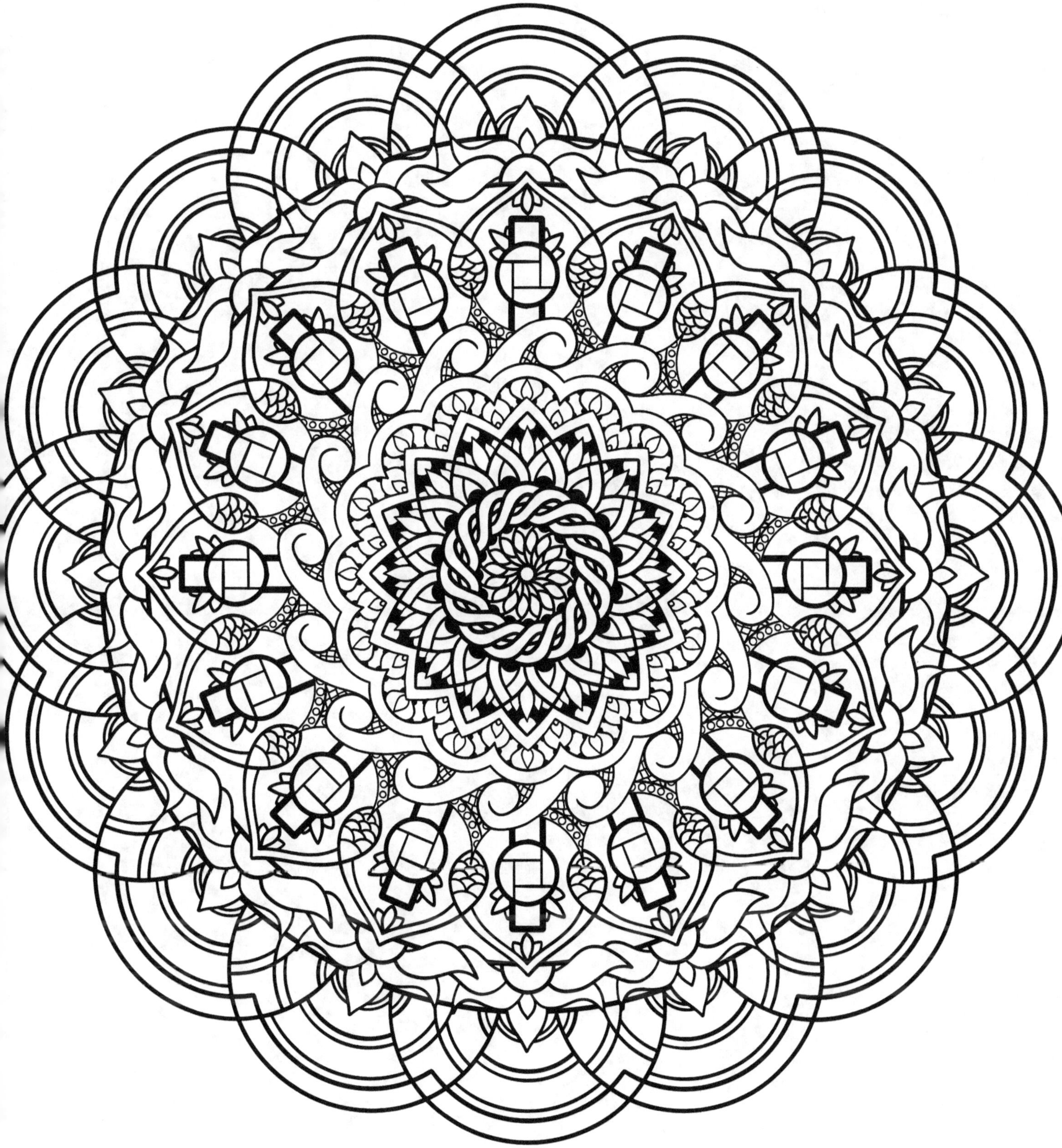

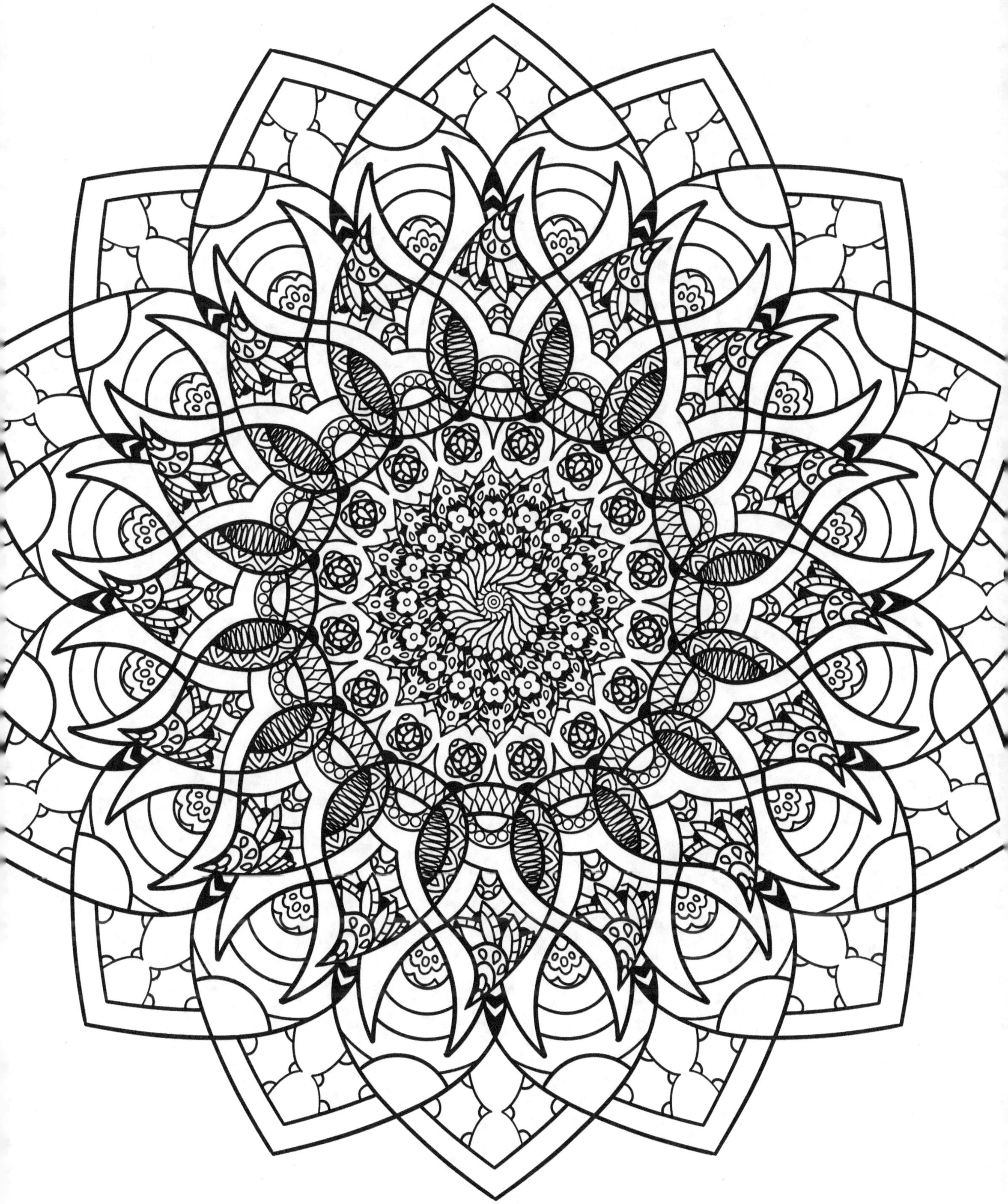

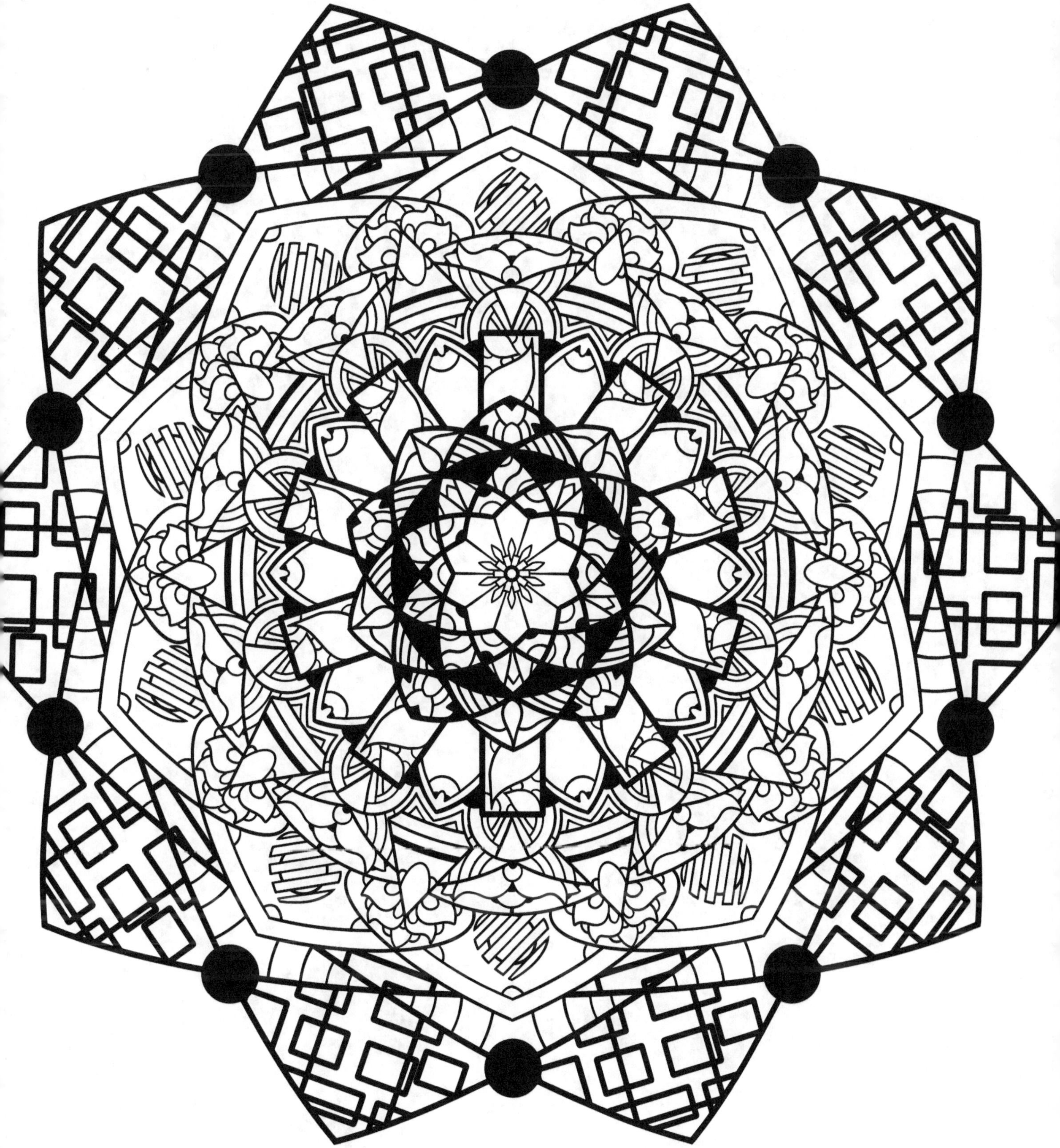

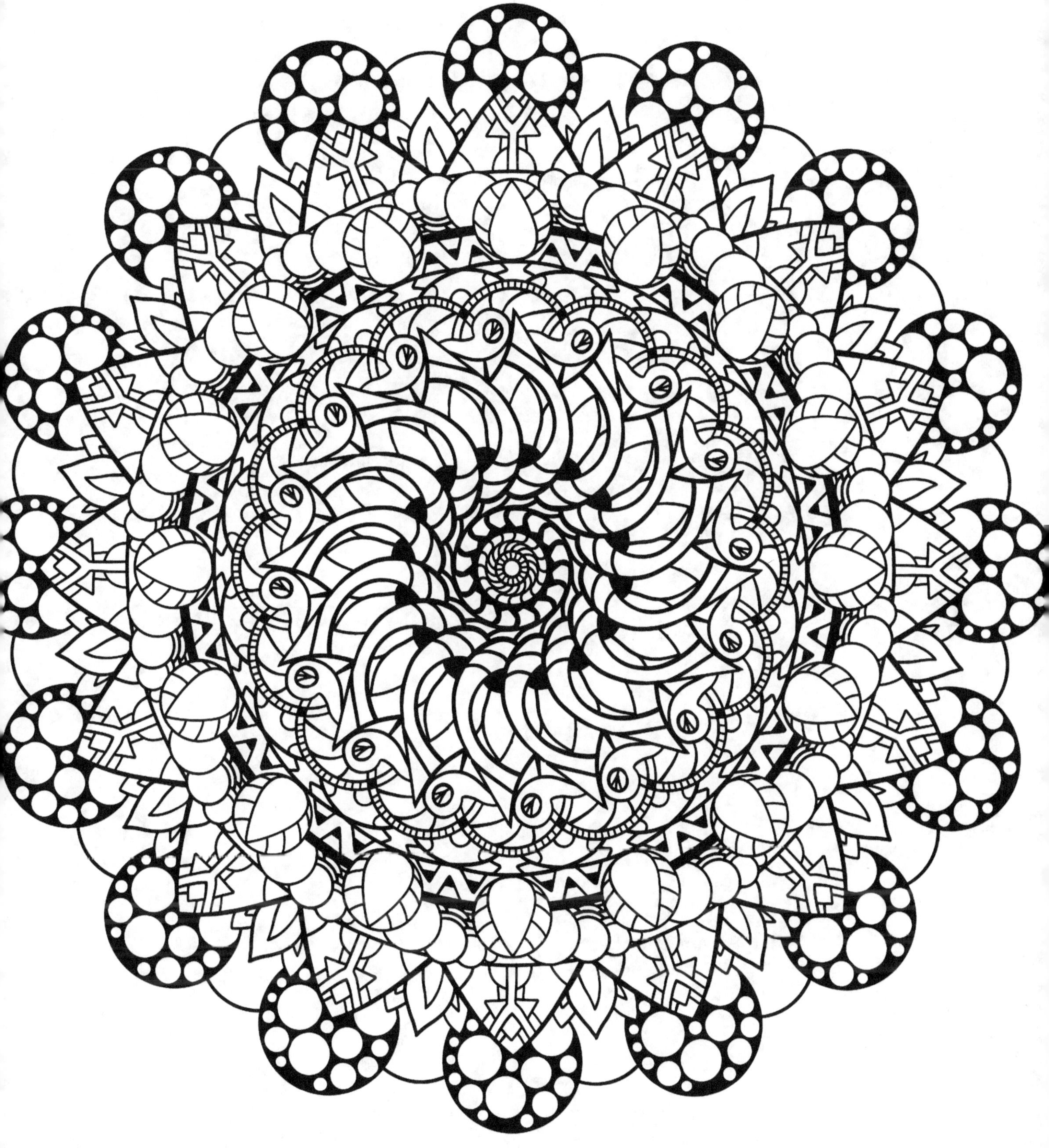

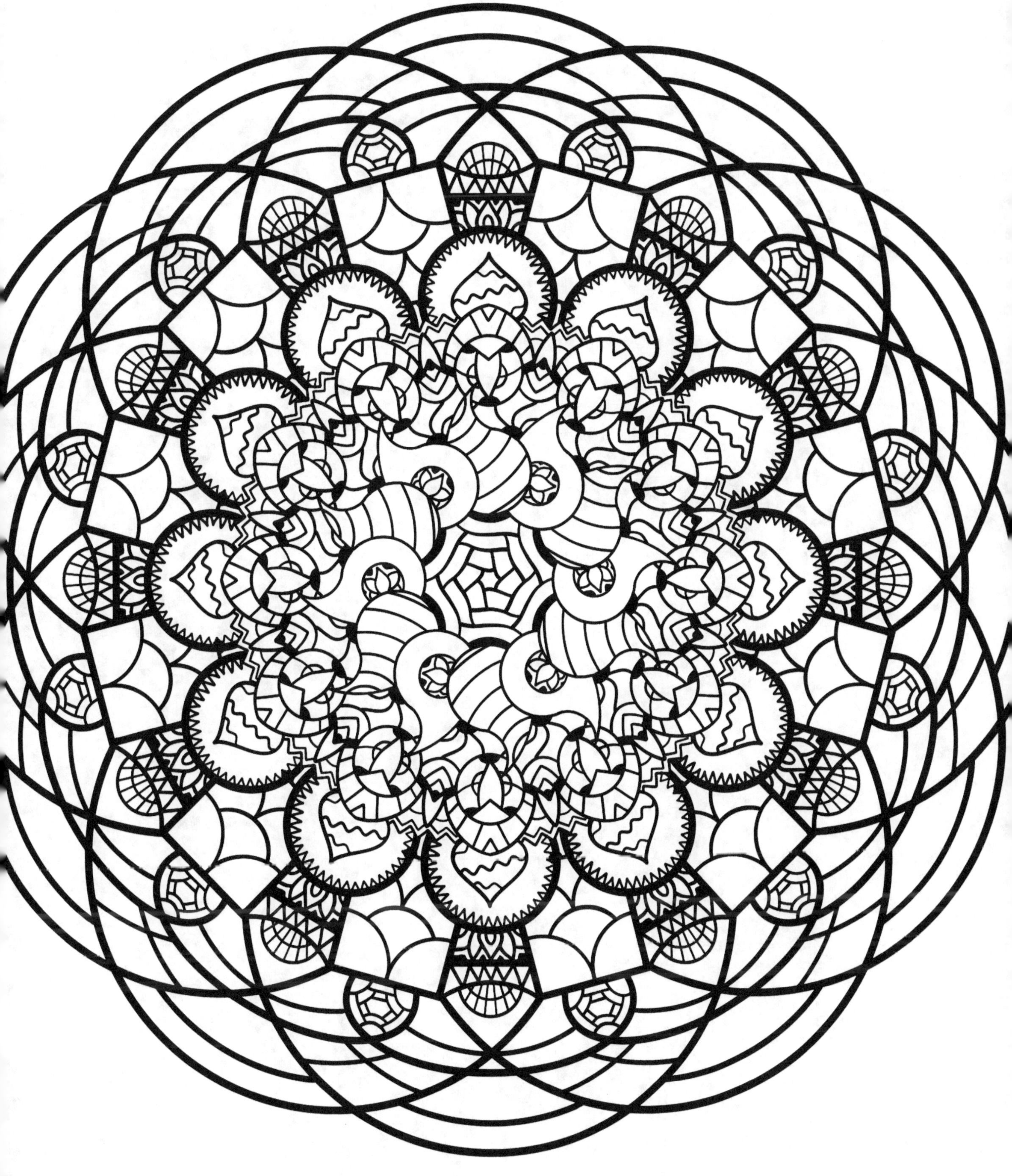

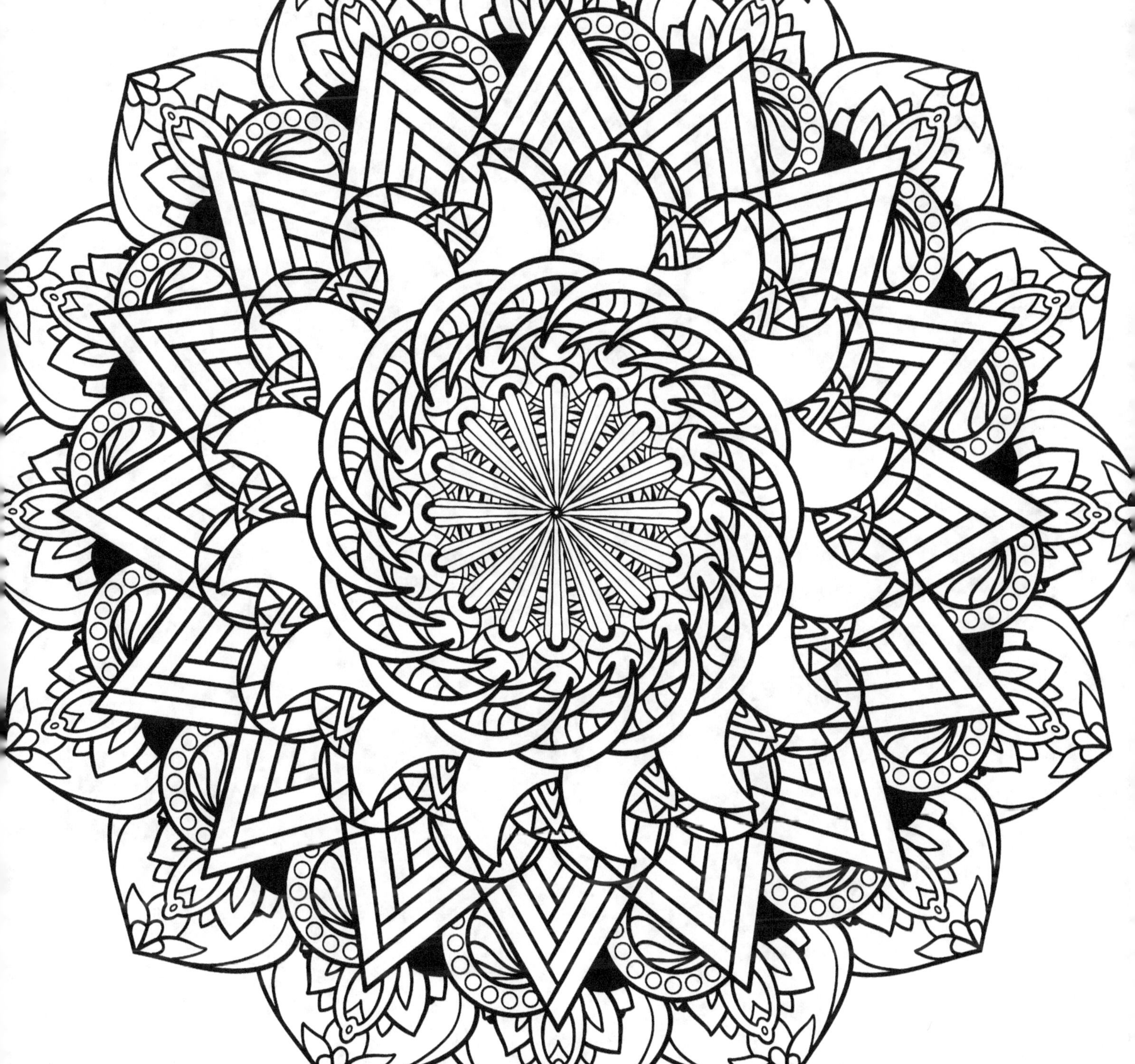

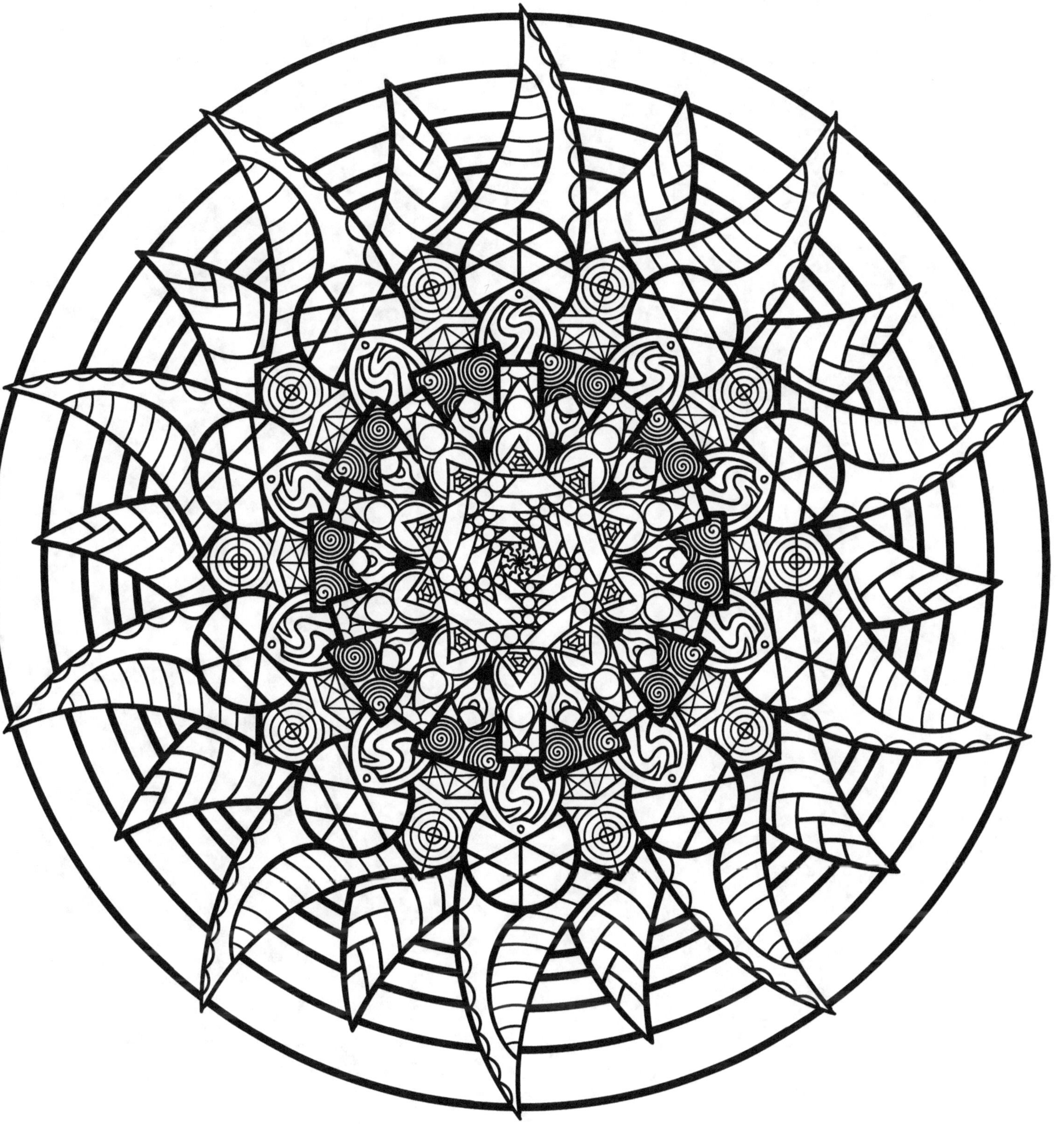

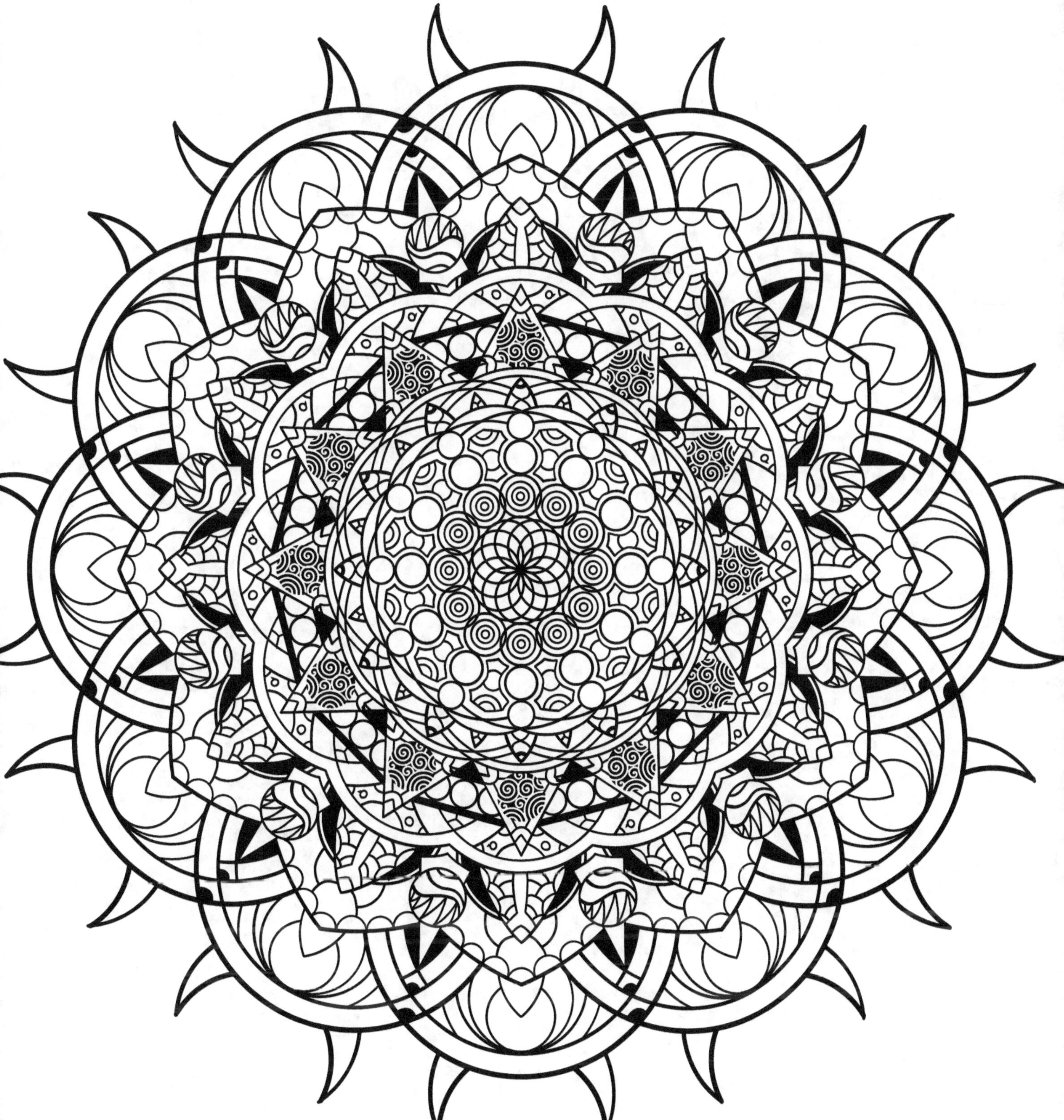

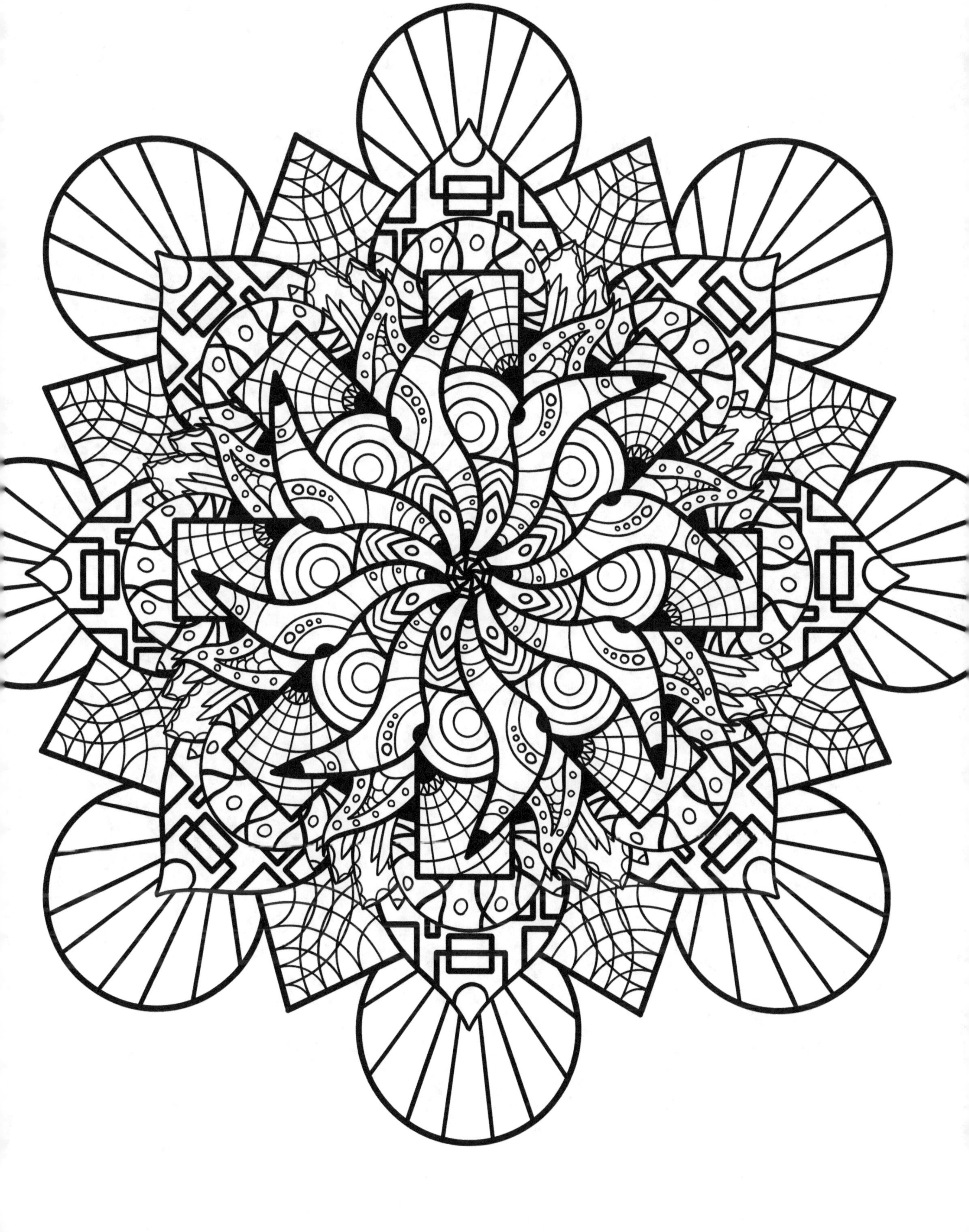

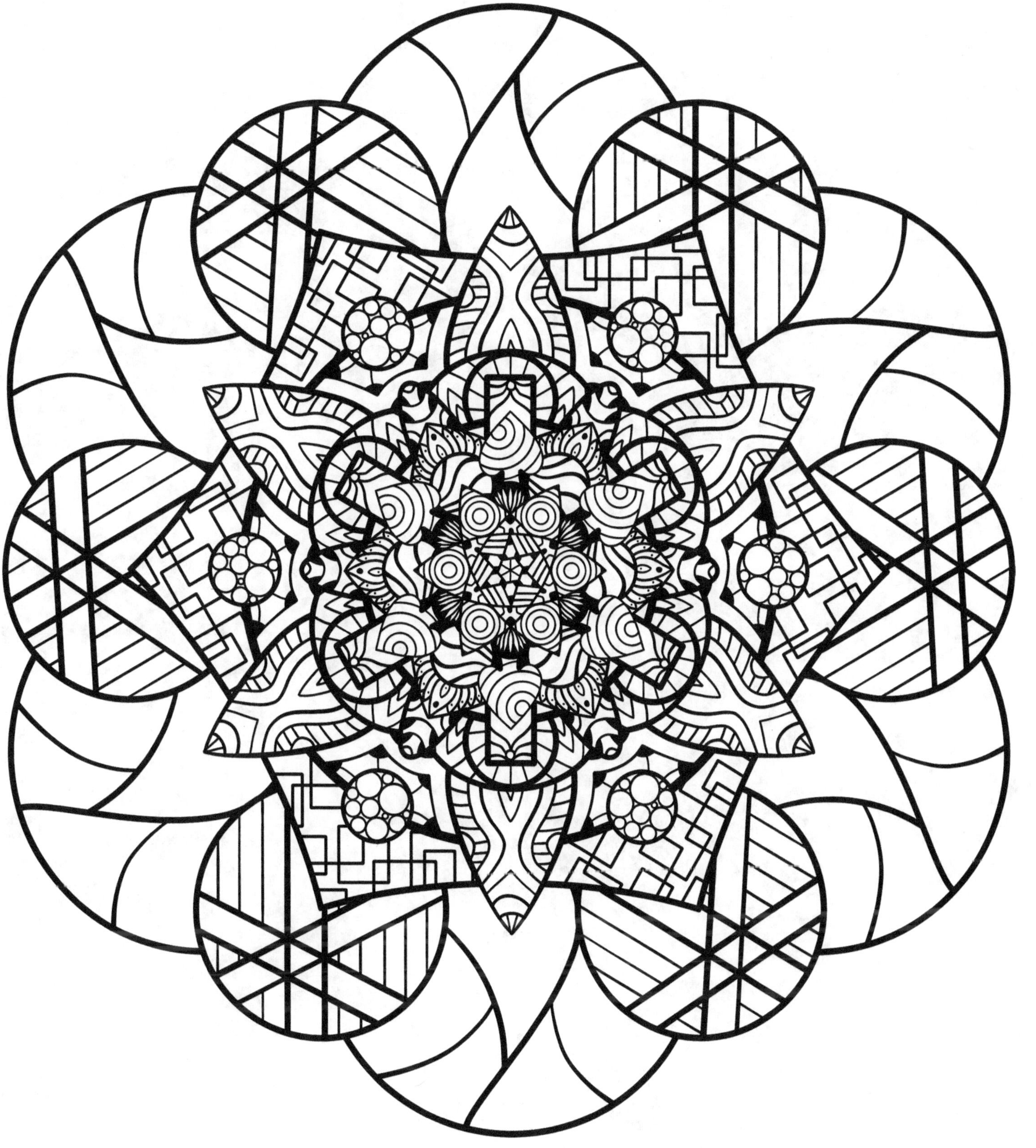

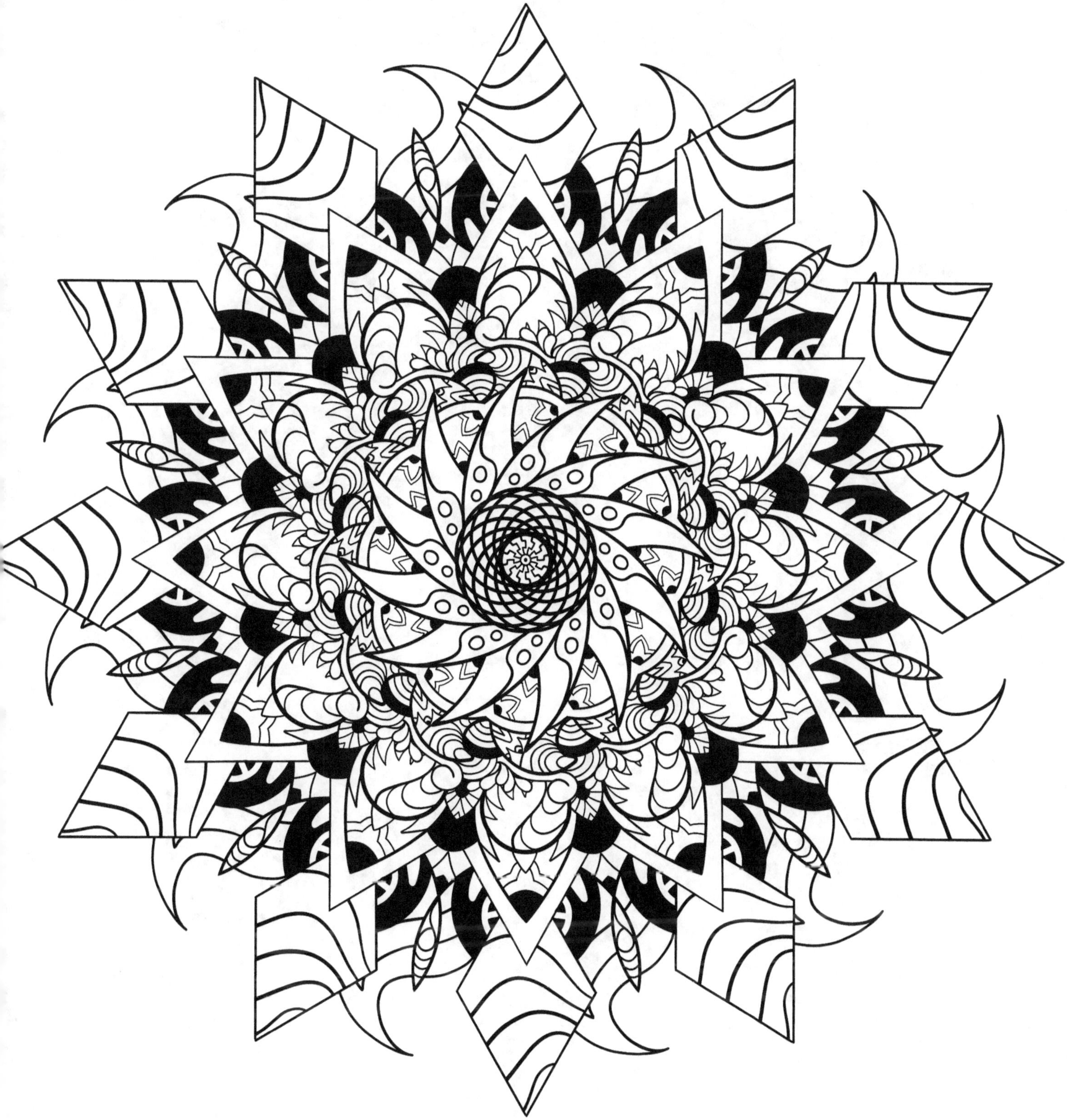

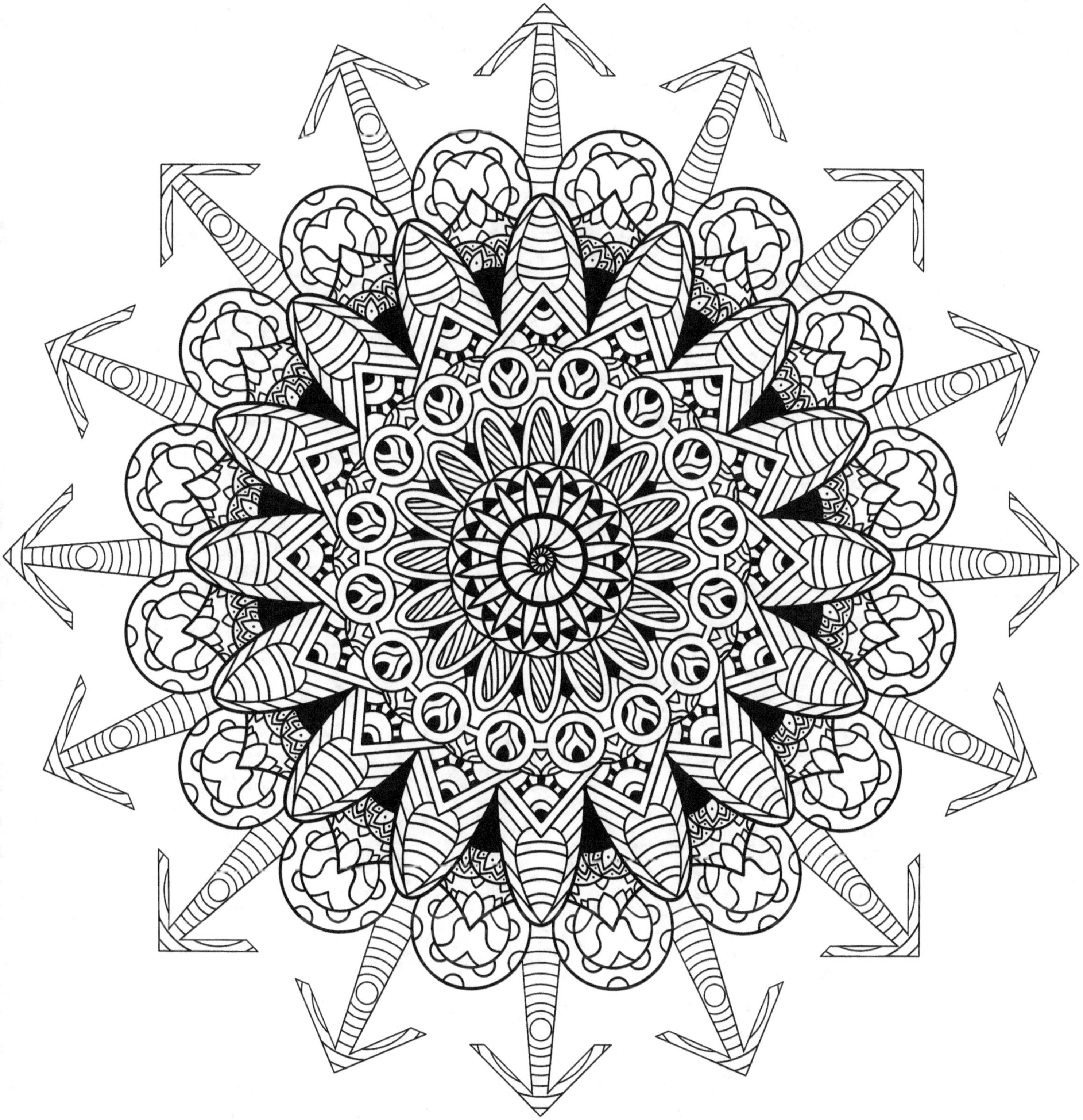

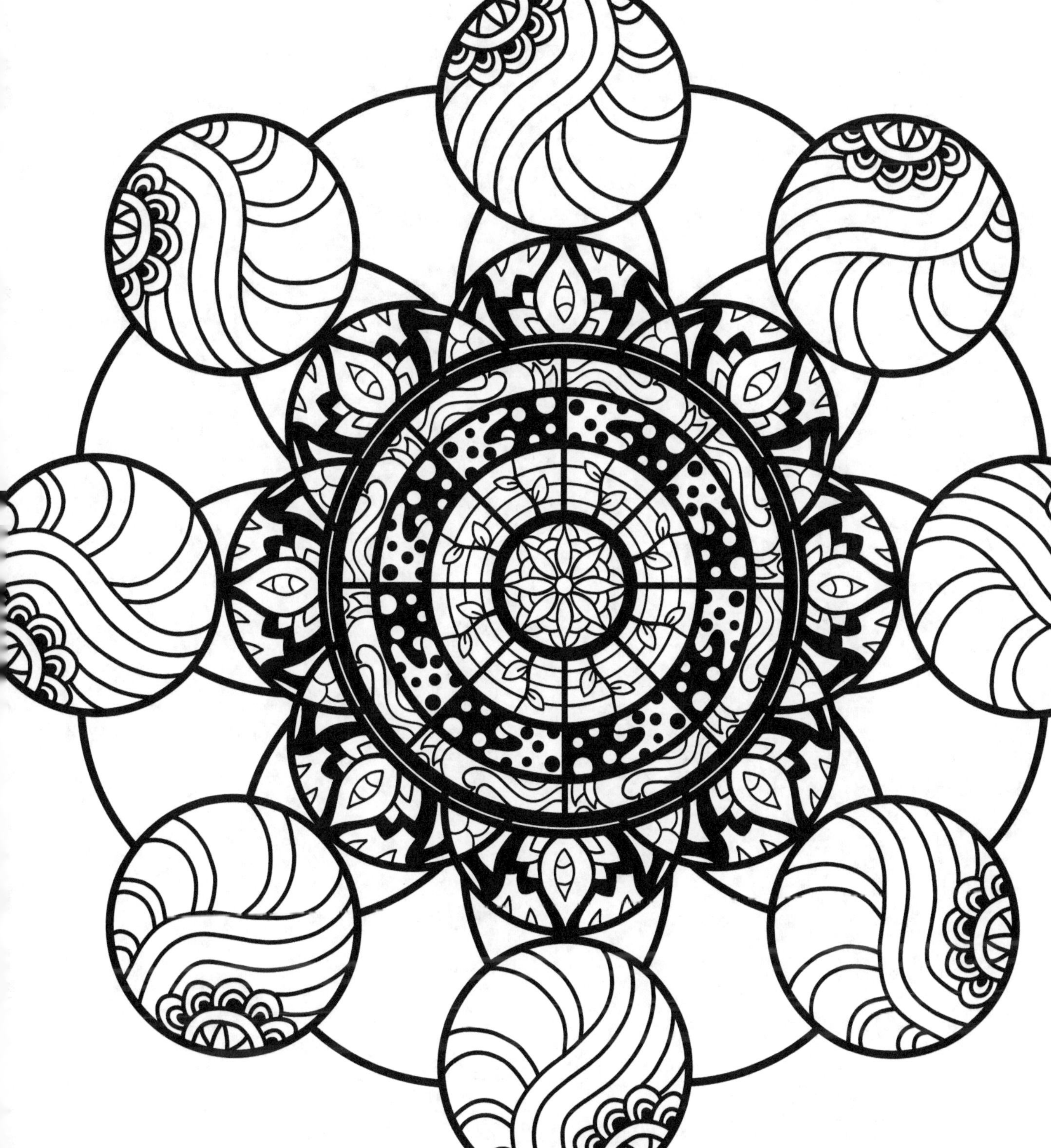

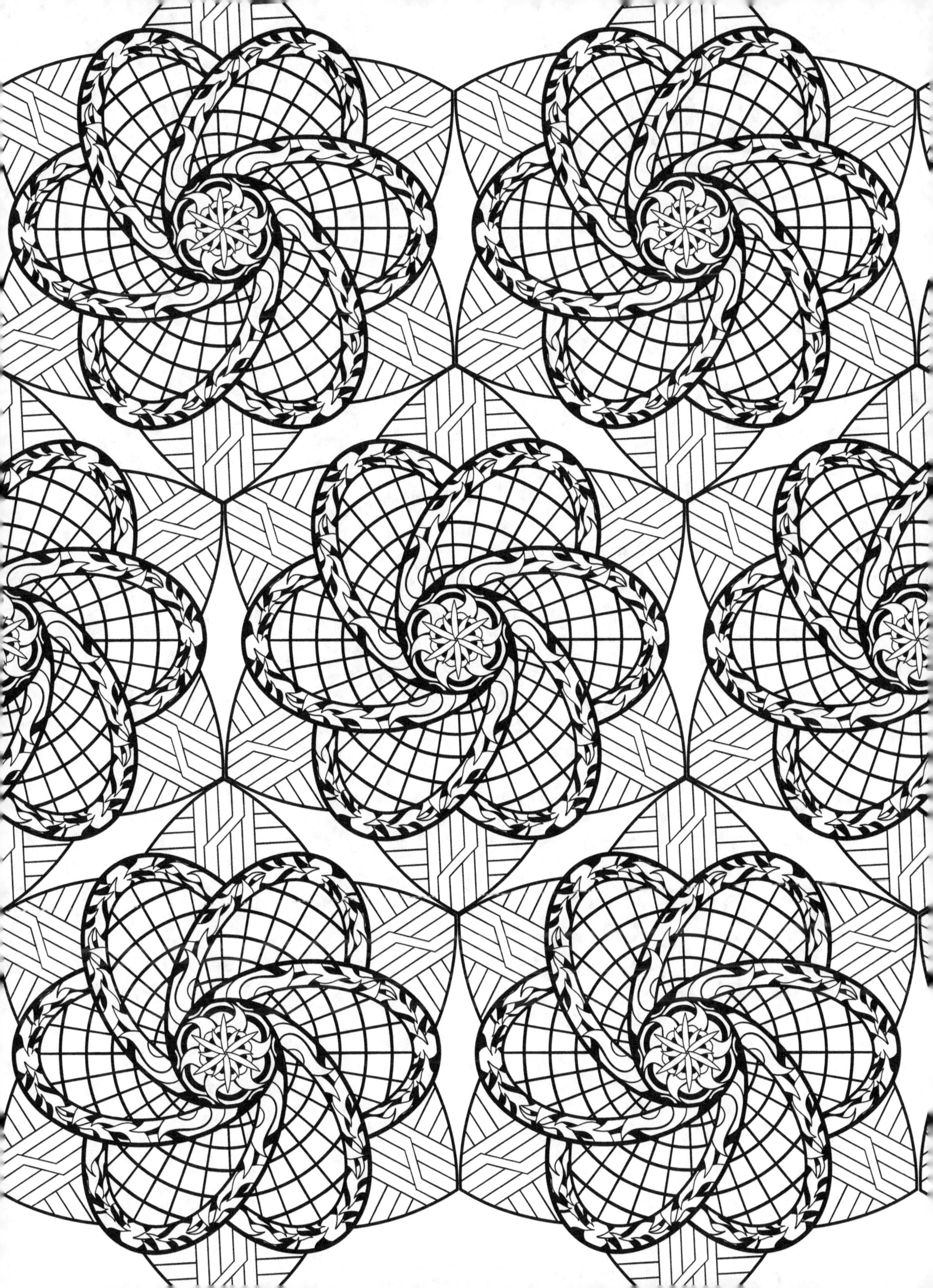

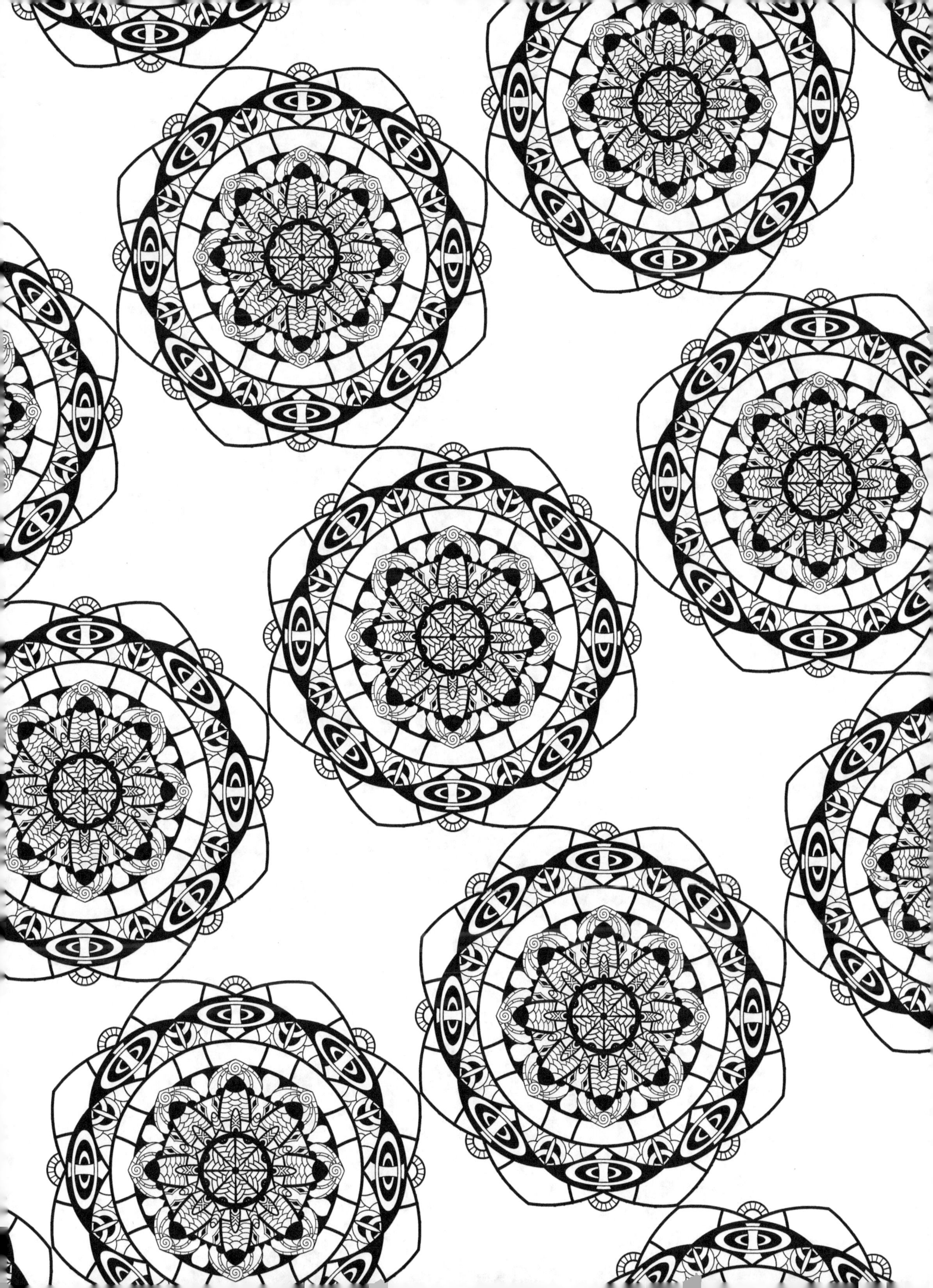

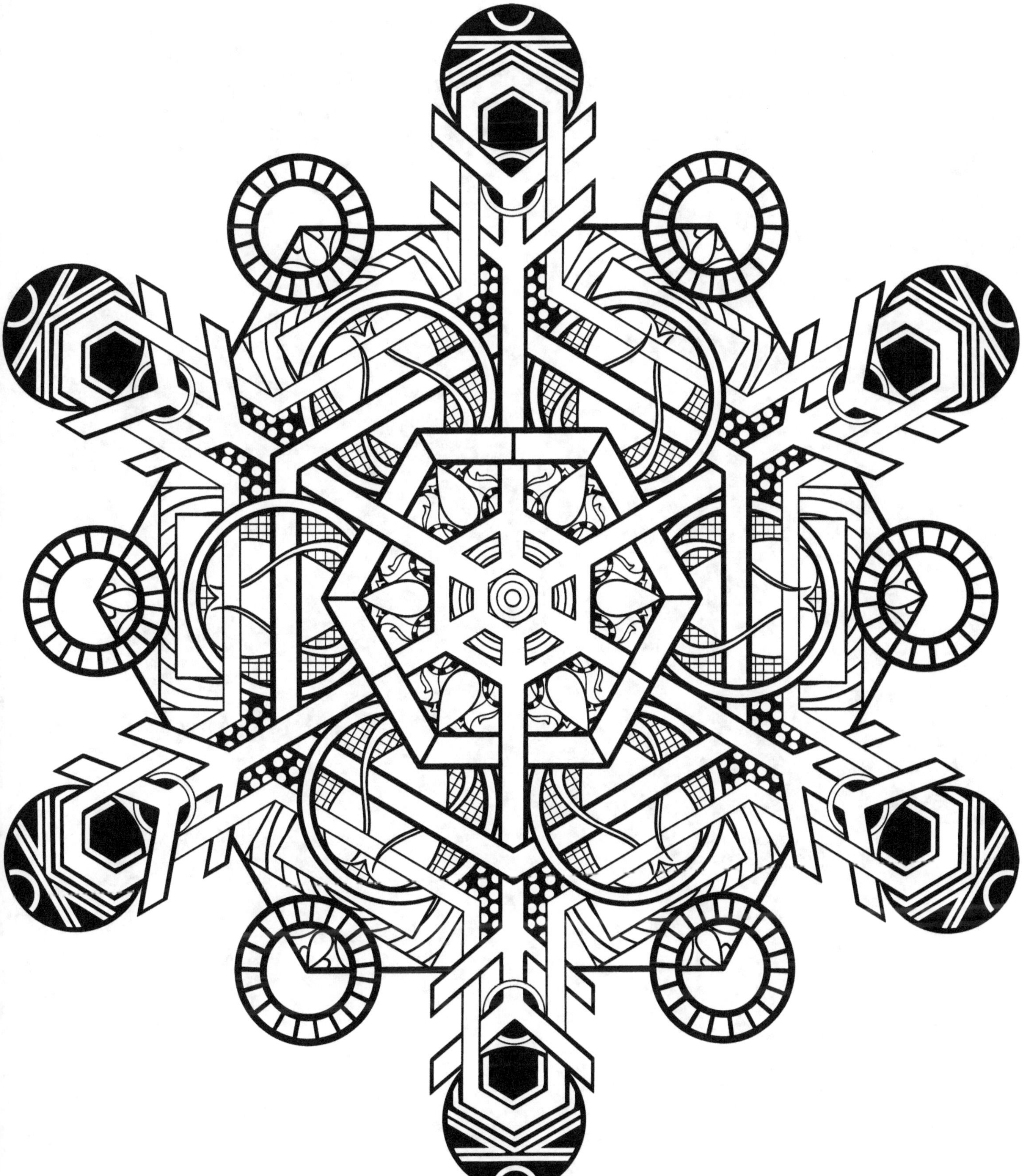

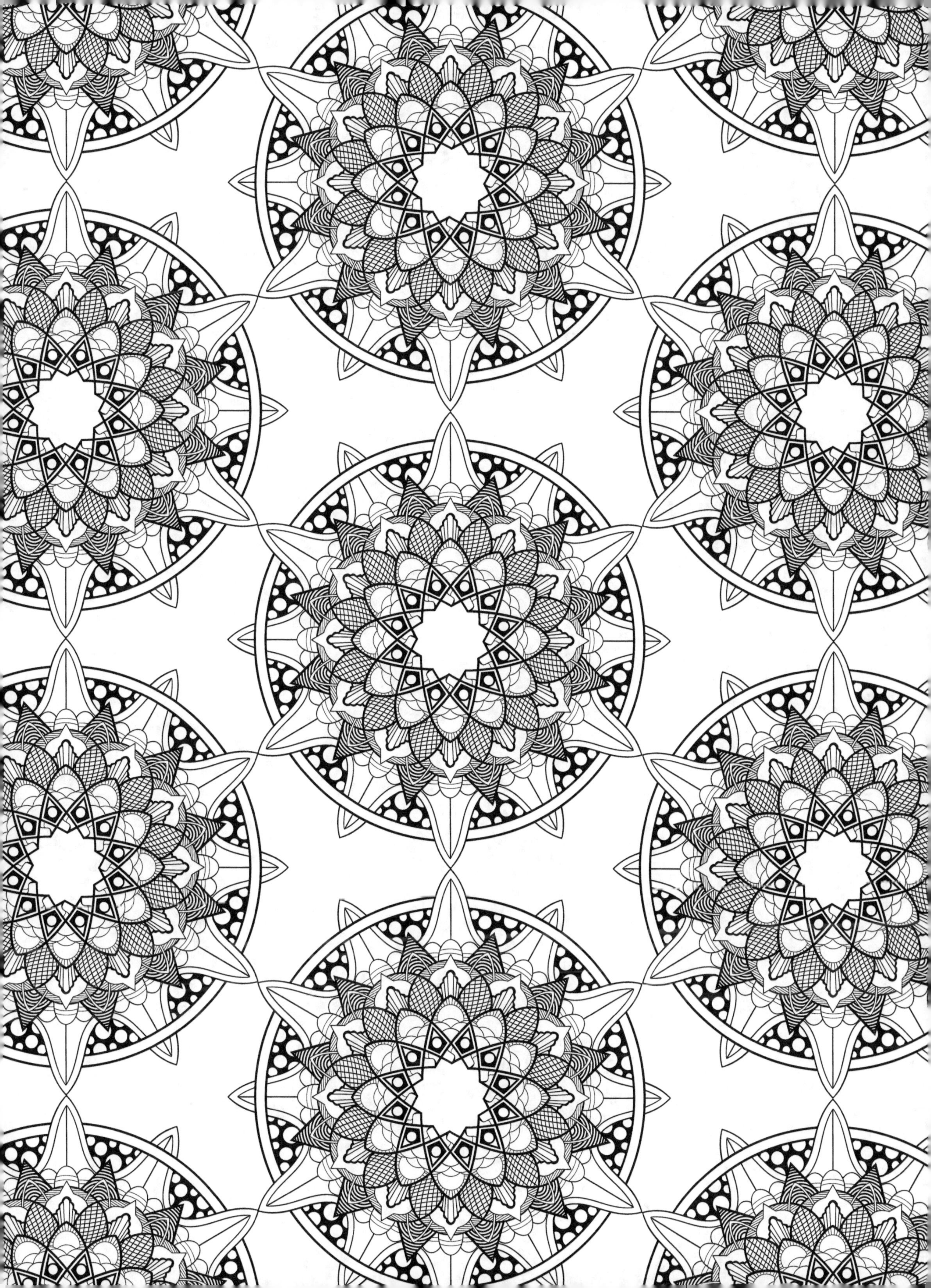

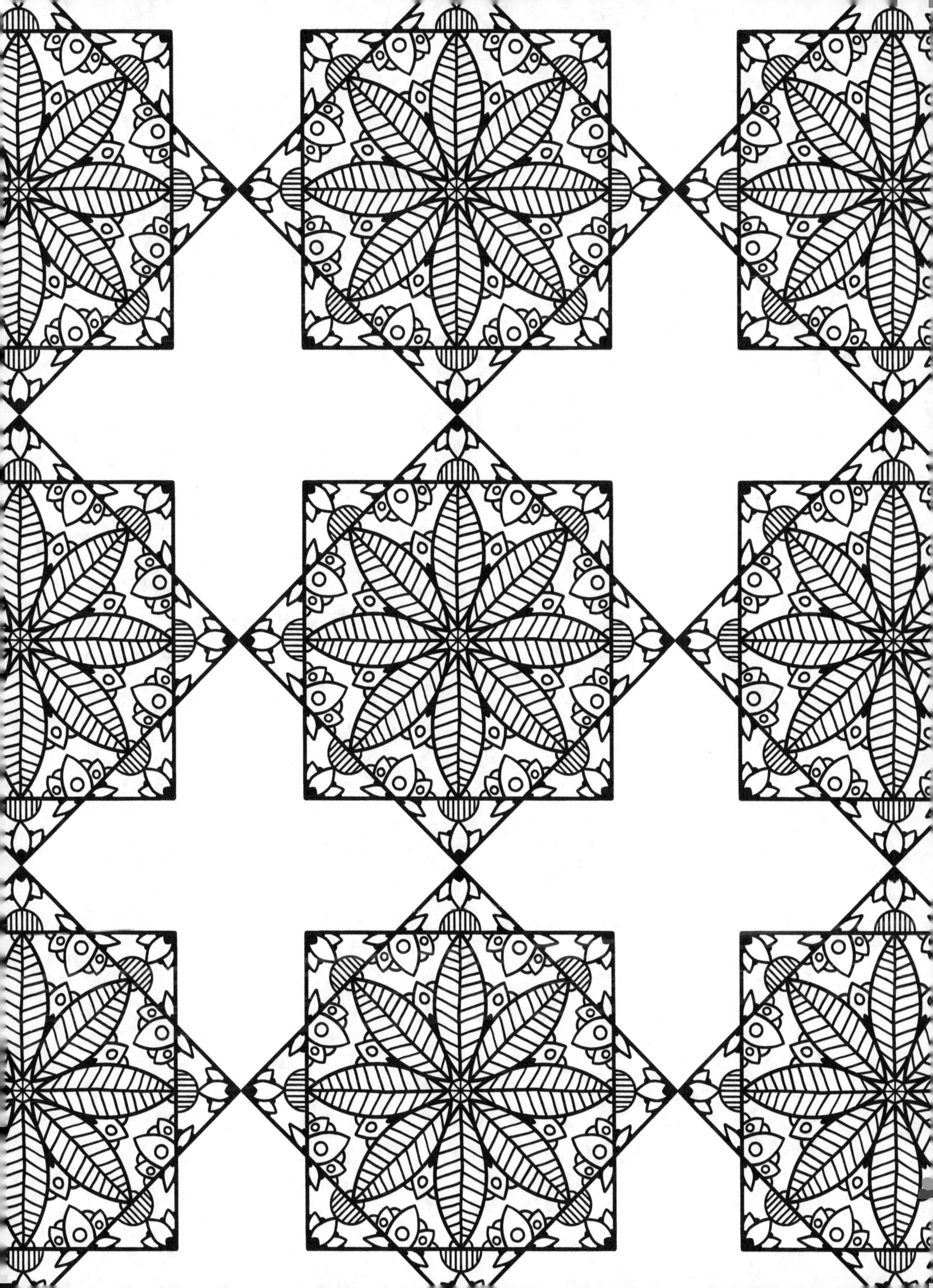

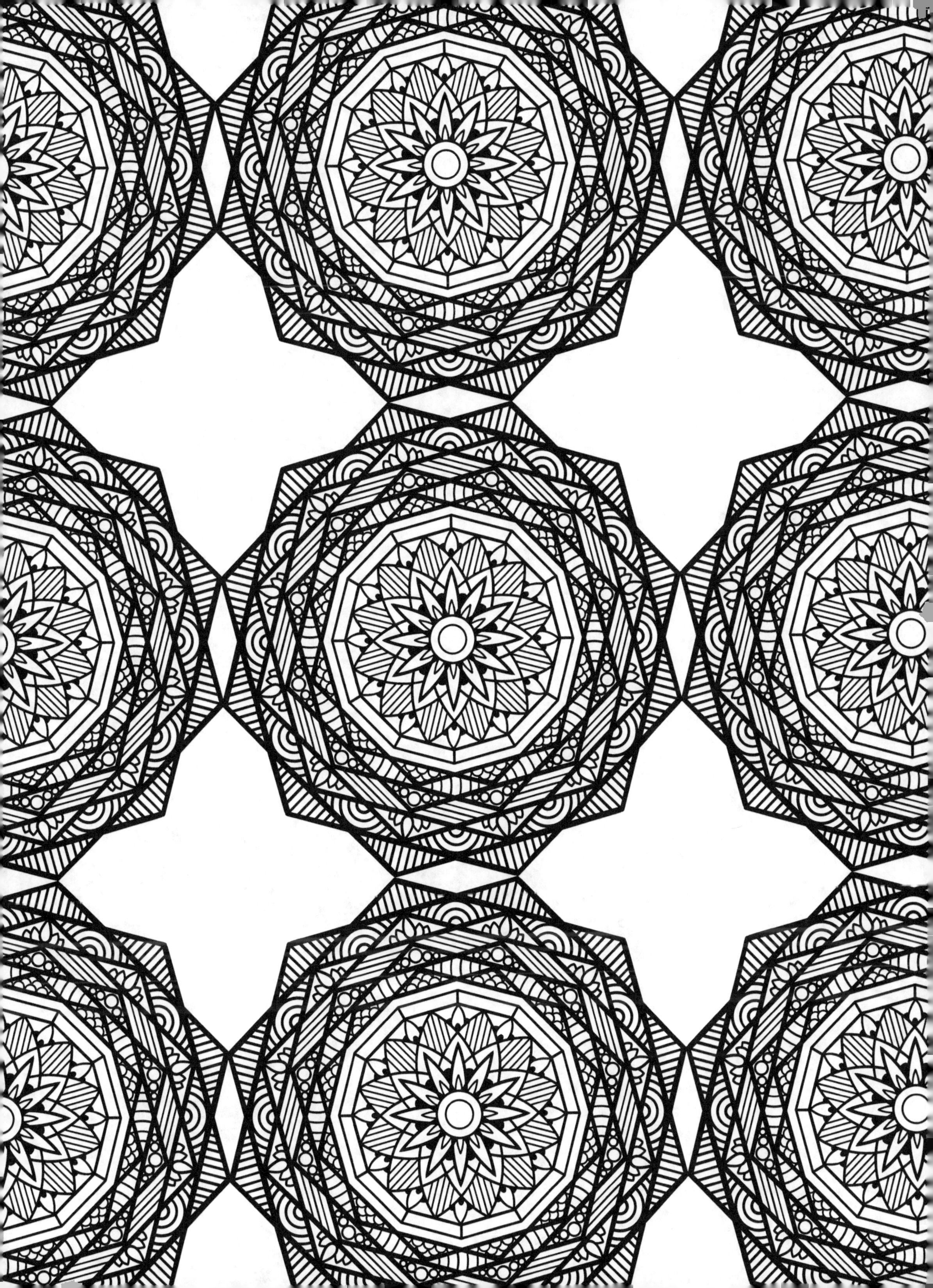

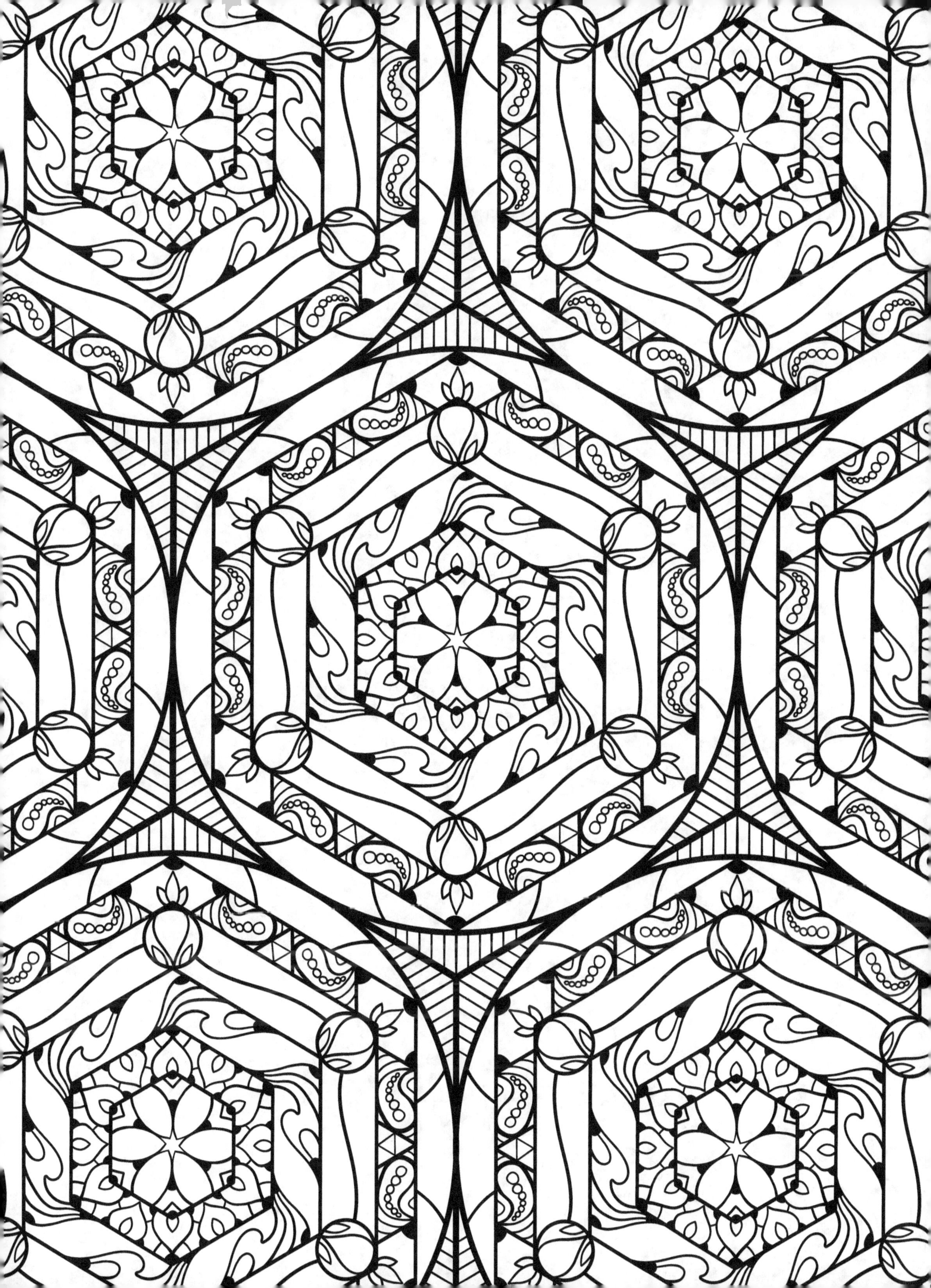

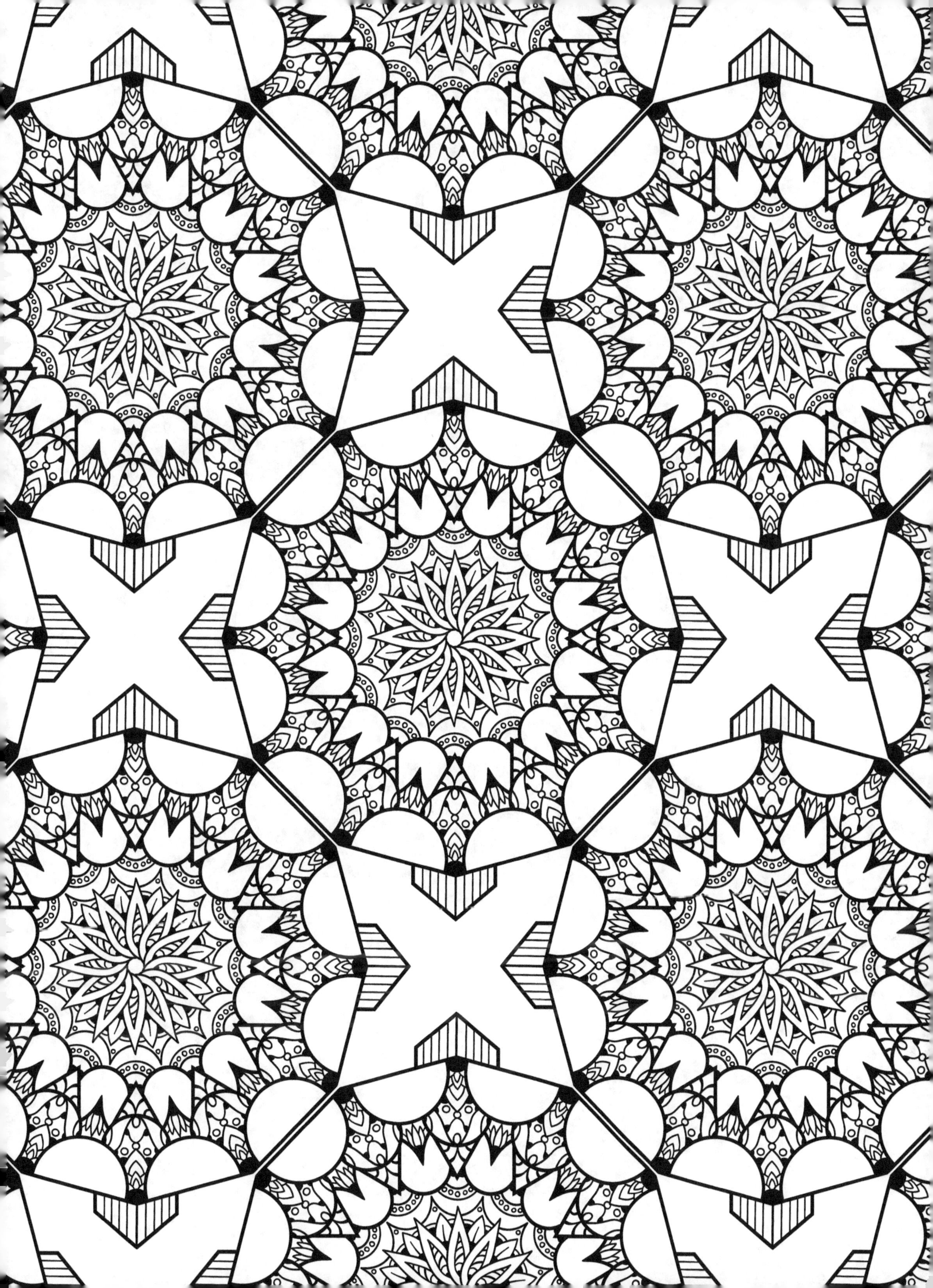

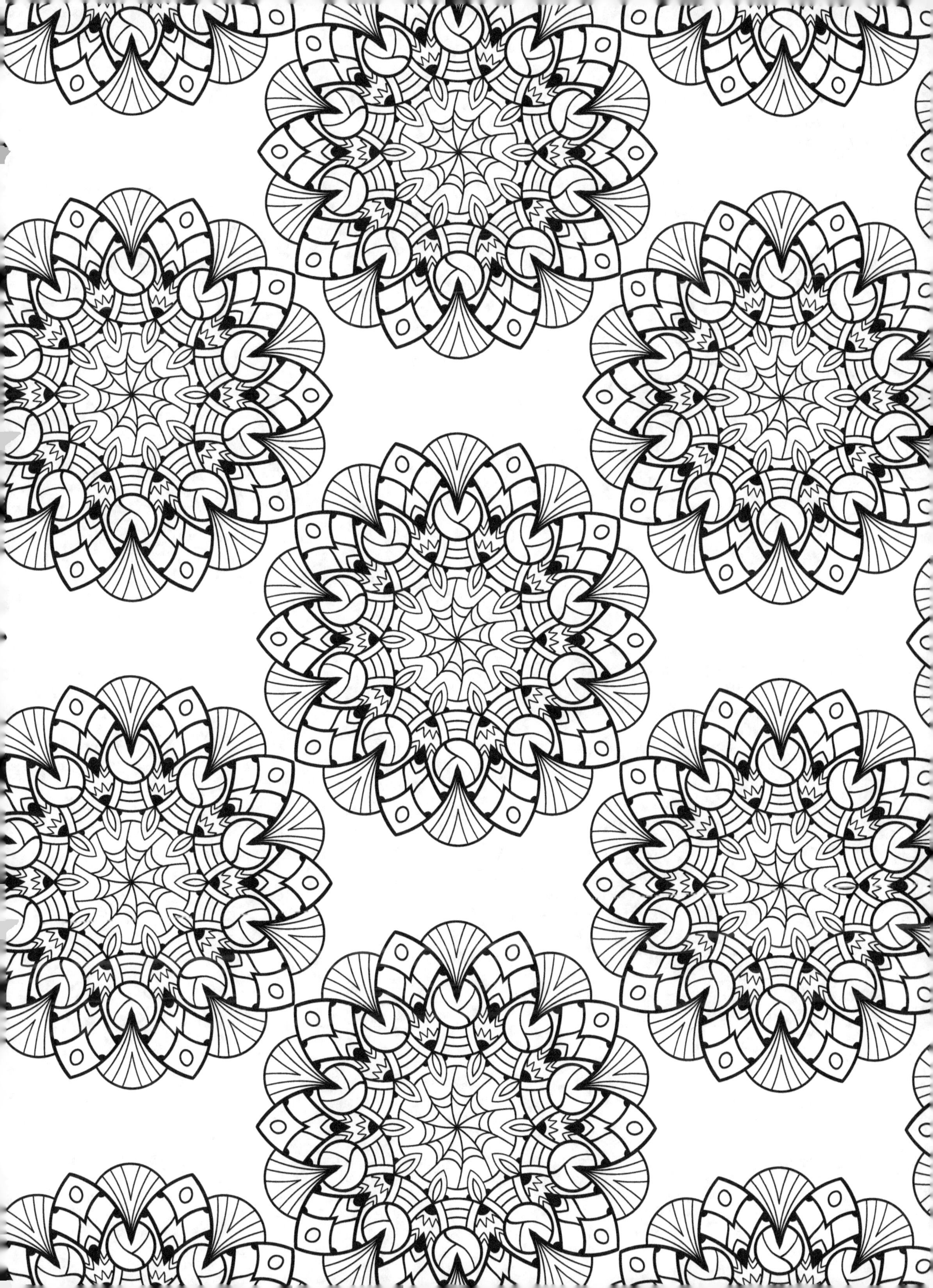

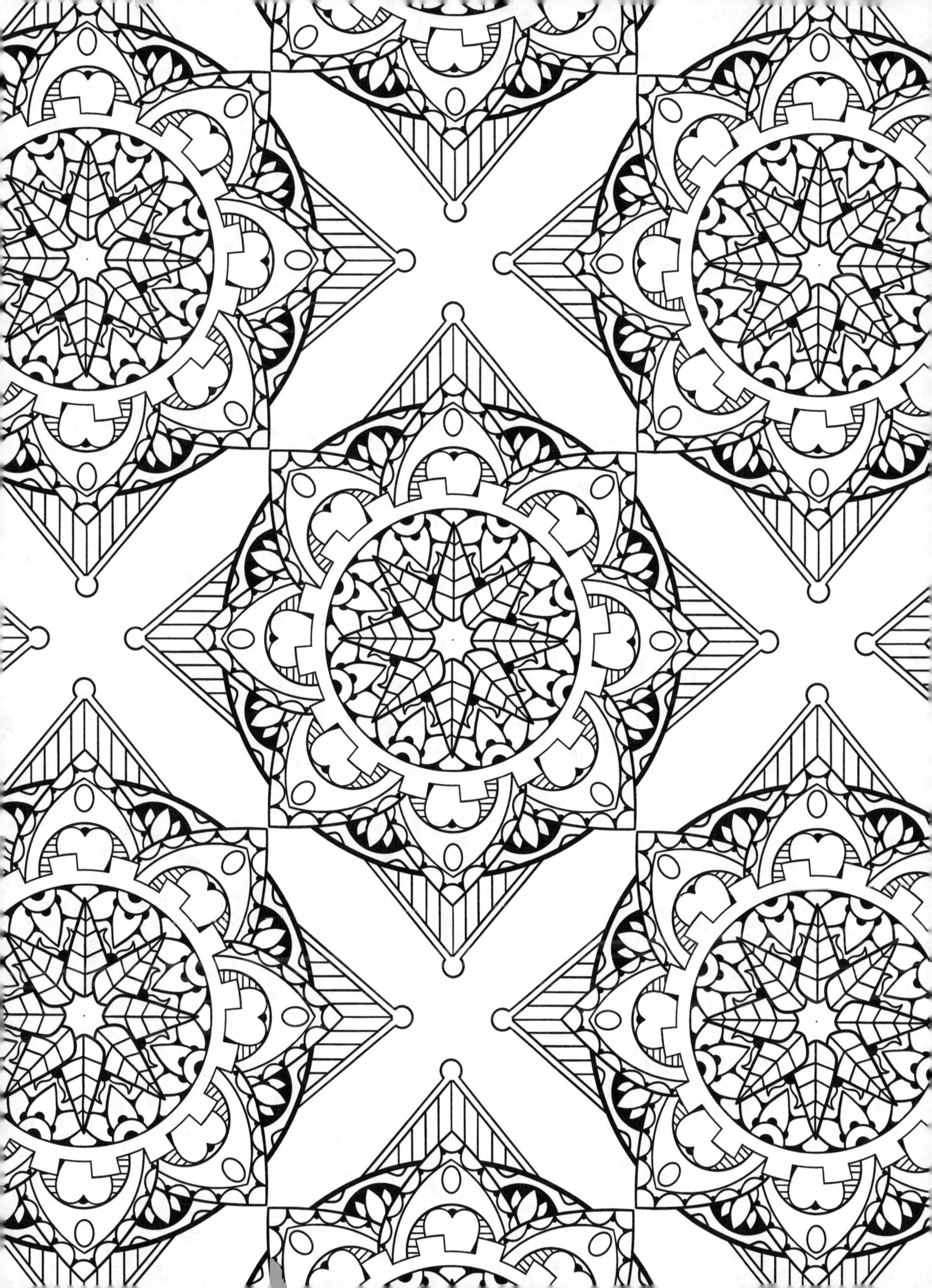

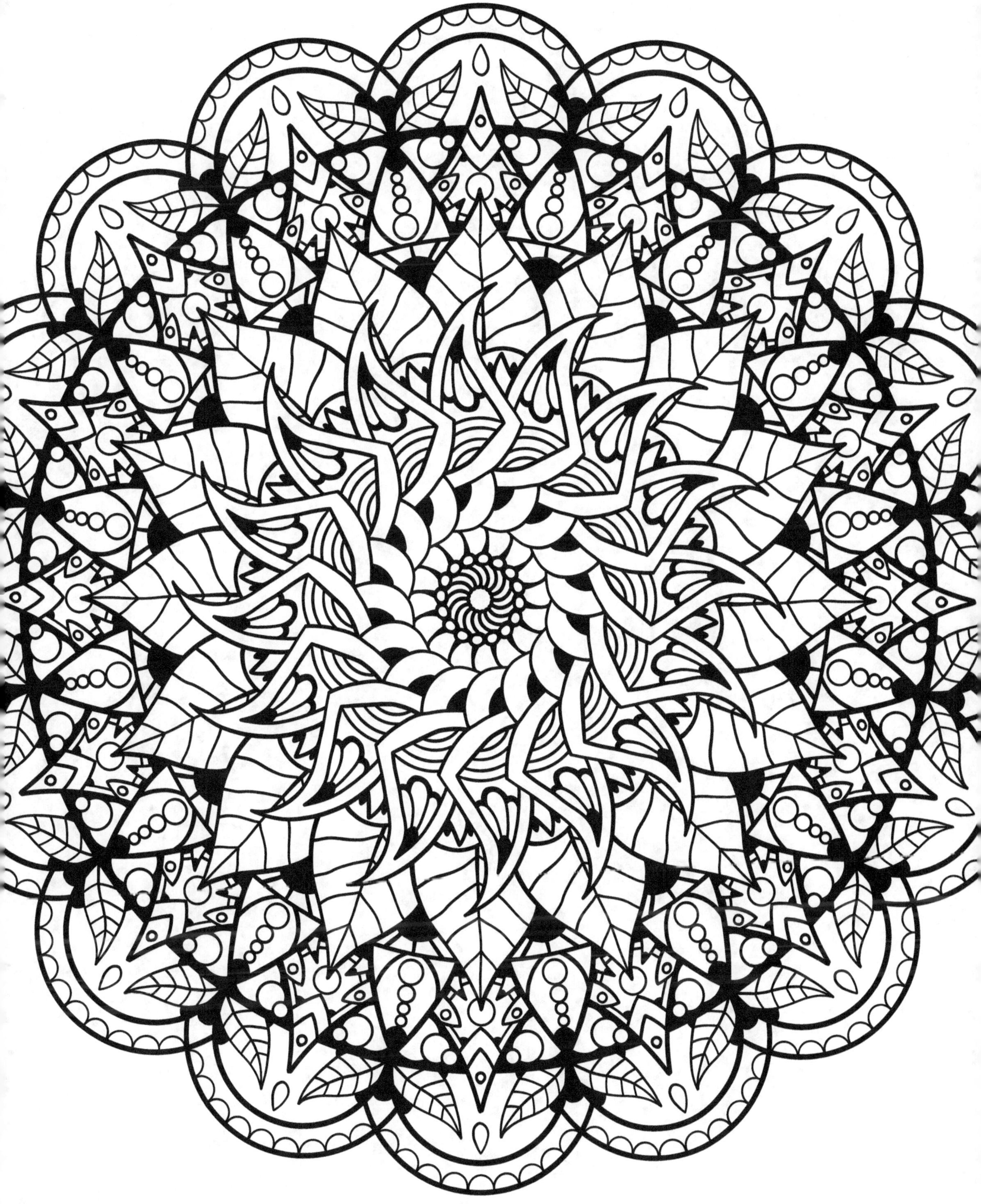

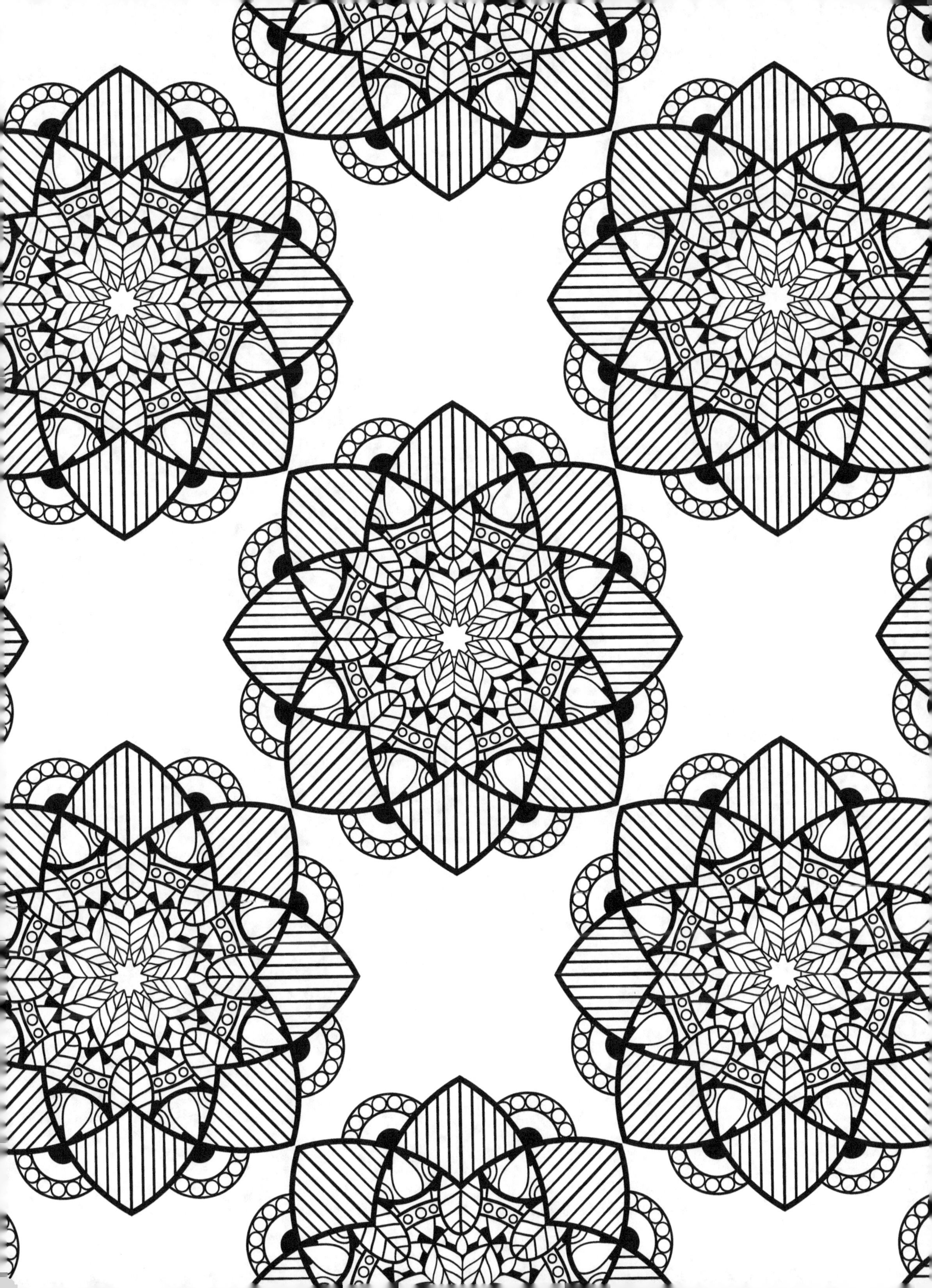

www.ingramcontent.com/pod-product-compliance
Lightning Source LLC
Chambersburg PA
CBHW081118180526
45170CB00008B/2907
* 9 7 8 1 5 3 9 9 8 9 7 6 9 *